THE PROZAC ALTERNATIVE

ᵀᴴᴱPROZAC ALTERNATIVE

Natural Relief from Depression
with St. John's Wort, Kava,
Ginkgo, 5-HTP, Homeopathy,
and Other Alternative Therapies

RAN KNISHINSKY

Healing Arts Press
Rochester, Vermont

Healing Arts Press
One Park Street
Rochester, Vermont 05767
www.InnerTraditions.com

Healing Arts Press is a division of Inner Traditions International

Copyright © 1998 by Ran Knishinsky

Note to the reader: This book is intended as an informational guide. The remedies, approaches, and techniques described herein are meant to supplement, and not to be a substitute for, professional medical care or treatment. They should not be used to treat a serious ailment without prior consultation with a qualified health-care professional.

Library of Congress Cataloging-in-Publication Data

Knishinsky, Ran, 1971–
    The prozac alternative : natural relief from depression with St. John's wort, kava, ginkgo, 5-HTP, homeopathy and other alternative therapies / Ran Knishinsky.
        p. cm.
    Includes bibliographical references and index.
    ISBN 0-89281-791-7 (pbk. : alk. paper)
    1. Depression, Mental—Alternative treatment—Popular works.   2. Depression, Mental—Nutritional aspects—Popular works.   3. Herbs—Therapeutic use—Popular works.   4. Fluoxetine—Popular works.   I. Title.
        RC537.K595   1998
    616.85'2706—dc21   98-25770
                                                          CIP

Printed and bound in the United States

10 9 8 7 6 5 4 3 2 1

Text layout by Bill Brilmayer
This book was typeset in Caslon with
Minion and Wade Sans Light as the display typefaces

ACKNOWLEDGMENTS

I would like to thank Fred Deutsch for his tireless computer and technical assistance; Melanie Chenet, R.Ph., for her knowledge; Alan Christianson, N.M.D., for his interview and help; editors Jon Graham, Rowan Jacobsen, and Blake Maher at Inner Traditions; copyeditor Lee Wood; Robin Straus, my literary agent; Elizabeth Ripley, for her great dependability and loyalty; Alma Loya, for her love and continued support; and Mira and Avi Knishinsky, my wonderful parents. Thanks to all the people at Inner Traditions International involved with this project. And deepest gratitude to the researchers who have labored intensely to discover the mysteries of St. John's wort and bring them to the public eye, including the writers of the St. John's wort monograph. If it were not for them, this book probably would never have been written.

CONTENTS

Chapter 1

The Focus Is on St. John's Wort

St. John's wort is already the favored therapy for depression in Germany, where it has been used therapeutically for centuries. Prepared as a tea, the herb was taken to calm frazzled nerves and revive a depressed spirit. It was also made into oil, which was sometimes used topically to relieve skin problems.

True to its folklore, an assortment of new clinical studies report that St. John's wort provides measurable relief to people with mild and moderate depression without the side effects of drugs like Prozac.[1] German doctors prescribed roughly sixty-six million daily doses of St. John's wort in 1994 for the relief of depression and anxiety. Classified as an approved medication in Germany, most of these doctors turn to the standard antidepressants only when the herbal remedy fails to take effect.[2] Apparently, their patients prefer it that way: the herb is currently outselling Prozac twenty to one in Germany.

St. John's wort vaulted to international fame after several well-respected scientific journals published articles on this herb's potential use in the treatment of clinical depression. In 1994 the *Journal of Geriatric Psychiatry and Neurology* devoted an entire issue—seventeen research papers in all—to "Hypericum: A Novel Antidepressant." One compelling study tracked the herb's effects on 3,250 patients battling mostly mild and moderate depression and found that about 80 percent either felt better or became completely free of symptoms after four weeks.[3] It further outlined the various pros and cons associated with the administration of the herb and summarized its remarkable effectiveness in battling depression.

This herb has been the subject of incredible amounts of recent mass media attention. The focus of thousands of published articles across the entire United States, it has appeared in newspapers from the *New York Times* to the *Los Angeles Times* and in countless local papers across the country. Major news organizations, including news channel CNN and *20/20* have aired features on the benefits of the herb. National magazines such as *Newsweek* and *U.S. News and World Report* have jumped on the herbal bandwagon as well. Dozens of Websites offer information on this herb every day. Health stores, supermarkets, and mass-market venues all advertise and sell St. John's wort.

"Until three months ago, I had never heard of hypericum," writes Michael A. Jenike, M.D., in an editorial for the *Journal of Geriatric Psychiatry and Neurology*, "but in reviewing these papers and other literature, I have been impressed with the potential of this compound as a therapeutic agent in the treatment of mild-to-moderate depressive illnesses, the kind of depressions that predominate in out-patient medical practices. The results of the many studies outlined in this Supplement form an impressive body of evidence indicating that hypericum may well be a potentially useful agent to treat mild-to-moderate depression."[4] In 1996 the *British Journal of Medicine* published a review of twenty-three controlled studies involving 1,757 depressed patients. In that analysis, researchers from the United States and Germany found that St. John's wort worked nearly three times better than a placebo.[5] The study demonstrated that the herb is just as effective as certain prescription antidepressants for treating mild and moderate depression—and sometimes more effective. It is also without the many side effects common among prescribed antidepressants such as Prozac and its close relative Paxil. Furthermore, it is less expensive. Prozac costs, on average, one hundred dollars a month, while St. John's wort, on the less expensive side, costs only about fifteen dollars a month. For someone on a tight budget, the herbal remedy may be a lifesaver. In addition, it is easily accessible since it is readily available without a prescription.

This all comes as good news to mental health professionals and patients. It finally looks as though a suitable alternative to prescription antidepressants may really exist. While prescription antidepressants are certainly effective and helpful for some, many others find St. John's wort a blessing. Thanks to the willingness of the scientific community to engage in alternative studies of herbal medications, more people can be put at ease. An alternative means of treating depression and anxiety is here.

St. John's Wort by Any Other Name

Like most herbs, St. John's wort has several names. No one is quite sure how the herb acquired its name, but several tales have evolved across the ages. The most obvious explanation is that the herb was named after St. John the Baptist, one of the holy figures in Christianity. *Wort* is an old English word for plant. Legends tell us that the herb which flowers around June 24, the date St. John was beheaded, sprang from his blood. The red pigment of the plant is believed by some to represent the blood of the saint. Other stories claim the knights of St. John of Jerusalem used the herb to treat the wounds that they suffered on the Crusade battlefields.[6] Despite the questionable authenticity of the myths, they have persisted throughout many centuries, and each myth, in its own symbolic manner, offers us a greater vision of the healing purposes of the herb.

The Latin name of the plant is *Hypericum perforatum,* and the herb often referred to as hypericum. *Hypericum* stems from the Greek word *ereikē,* "heather," with the prefix *hypo,* "under," thus, a low-growing form of heather. *Perforatum* is translated as "punctured" and refers to the many tiny black-red dots that cover the leaves and flowers.[7] In the sunlight, it appears as if the flower petals are perforated. A surefire way to recognize St. John's wort is to rub the flowers and leaves between your fingers. If blood-red oil dyes your skin, then you can be certain you have correctly identified the herb. Believers in the doctrine of signatures, an ancient theory that every plant bears a clear sign of its use, once interpreted the tiny red dots as symbolic of blood, indicating St. John's wort's usefulness as a wound healer. Herbalists comment that the black-red spots contain the essential oils and resins responsible for the greater portion of its medicinal actions.

From ancient times through the Middle Ages, people thought St. John's wort possessed supernatural powers, using it to defend themselves against disease and evil and to chase away the devil and ominous spirits.[8]

During the Middle Ages, illness was often attributed to evil spirits. Because St. John's wort was supposedly endowed with magical powers, the ingestion of the herb was believed to keep the spirits from attacking. On St. John's Eve it was burned in bonfires to purify the air and repel the spirits. The following poem, written around the year A.D. 1400, characterizes the medieval attitude toward the benevolent plant:

> St. John's wort doth charm all witches away
> If gathered at midnight on the saint's holy day.
> Any devils and witches have no power to harm
> Those that gather the plant for a charm.
> Rub the lintels with that red juicy flower;
> No thunder nor tempest will then have the power
> To hurt or hinder your house; and bind
> Round your neck a charm of a similar kind.[9]

Centuries ago, people believed that the herb was imbued with the essence of St. John the Baptist; its ability to heal was directly related to the healing spirit of God and the authority of his saint. Nowadays, our perspective on the mechanisms of medicinal plants assumes an entirely scientific tone. Because an herb's mechanism of action can be explained in scientific terms, it no longer is in need of elucidation in religious terms. We are aware that active components within the herb are responsible for its various therapeutic effects and that the body contains complex chemicals keenly responsive to those active constituents. Scientific explanations appear to render the ancient myths invalid. But on second thought, what if the myths are real? All myths certainly convey bits of truth. After all, science is only recently discovering what old-time herbalists have known for centuries.

THE OTHER TALENTS OF ST. JOHN'S WORT

St. John's wort has been sitting quietly on the shelves of health food stores for many years now, and no one gave it much attention until the recent clinical information was released. Since the new studies and articles primarily deal with St. John's wort as a treatment for depression, you may not have heard of its many other extraordinary claims to fame.

The therapeutic applications of hypericum are far-reaching. It is not only used for mood regulation, but is also recommended in the treatment of a wide range of physiological disorders. St. John's wort is valued as a natural antibiotic, anti-inflammatory, antiviral, wound healer, and pain reliever. Chapter 6 will take a look at the ailments this herb is reported to treat, in addition to examining the scientific evidence validating its use. In the meantime, I would like to tell you about some other recent studies that have drawn attention to the herb.

Two of the world's leading medical institutions, New York University Medical Center and the Weizman Institute of Science in Rechovot, Israel, reported that St. John's wort may be effective in treating HIV, the AIDS virus. They found that one of the herb's main constituents inhibits the growth of retroviruses in animals, including HIV.

Other clinical studies currently being conducted throughout the United States are investigating the use of St. John's wort as a treatment for cancer. So far, the results look good. A synthetic preparation of the herb is proving useful in the treatment of one the most deadly diseases of our time.

IS ST. JOHN'S WORT FOR YOU?

If you, or someone you know, is suffering from depression, St. John's wort may be of assistance. It has been dubbed the "natural Prozac" for good reason. Shown in clinical trials to be an effective treatment for varying degrees of depression, St. John's wort successfully relieves anxiety and insomnia as well—without dangerous or annoying side effects.

The herb continues to amaze researchers. One clinical study recently demonstrated that the herb might be influential in the treatment of Seasonal Affective Disorder (SAD), commonly referred to as the "winter blues." No prescription antidepressant has as many therapeutic applications as St. John's wort.

In Germany, where the bulk of the research on St. John's wort was conducted, the herbal remedy claims more than 50 percent of the antidepressant market, while Prozac claims only 2 percent.[10] In stark contrast to the situation in Germany, Prozac currently dominates the $6 billion worldwide market for antidepressants. St. John's wort is the first herbal treatment for depression that the medical establishment is taking seriously, and it has received the endorsements of several of the top medical and scientific journals. Even the medical establishment in the

United States is opening its doors to the herb: the National Institute of Mental Health is cofunding the country's first national study of St. John's wort.

Could a remarkable change in medicine be on the way? Is it possible that a shift from synthetic antidepressants to a more holistic approach might be in the works?

If you are excited by all this news, join the crowd. But do not throw away your Prozac, Paxil, or Zoloft before you read all the evidence. I will do my best throughout this book to provide you with an objective viewpoint on the herb, taking a discriminating look at all the evidence presently available on the nature and history of herbs, causes and symptoms of depression, natural and orthodox therapies, and the results of recent clinical studies.

CHAPTER 2

THE WAY OF HERBS

Herbs have always been an important part of medicine and were used by folk healers and physicians alike. The word *drug* is derived from the old Dutch word *drogee,* which means "to dry." Herbalists, pharmacists, and physicians used to dry their herbs as part of the preparation process. Currently, approximately 25 percent of all prescription drugs are still derived from shrubs, herbs, or trees. The World Health Organization notes that of 119 plant-derived pharmaceutical medicines, about 74 percent are used by modern medicine in ways that correlate directly with their traditional uses as plant medicines by native cultures.[1] Some of today's drugs are prepared from plant extracts, and others are synthetic derivatives that imitate the natural plant compounds.[2]

During the last several years, alternative medicine has made quite a comeback in the United States. Going beyond a "back to nature" fad or a rejection of conventional medicine, the field of natural medicine represents a yearning on the part of individuals to return to a more broad-based approach to medicine. Holistic medicine takes into account all the bodily systems and functions and is concerned with their balance. Holistic medicine recognizes that health should be more than simply the absence of sickness. Ancient healers viewed health as a balance between the person as a whole and the cosmos. When these forces became imbalanced, disease set in. This was the conceptual framework for medicine for a very long period of time. The germ theory of disease, introduced in the 1860s, transformed this age-old approach to medicine, and contemporary medicine, with its emphasis on infectious causes of disease, was born.[3] Toward the end of the nineteenth century, as this theory of medicine became more popular and gained greater support among the physicians and scientists of the world, it overshadowed the individual's own power to influence his or her health. With this shift in focus, illness was viewed as happenstance. In other words, illness just happened to people and there was nothing you could really do about it. The high-tech medicine that evolved tended to treat diseases rather than individuals and never really emphasized the preventive aspect of health.

Today, of course, we have a more moderate view of sickness and health. We realize that there are certain conditions that predispose one to being ill, just as there are conditions that predispose one to being healthy. We know that most diseases result from a complex combination of factors; no one factor causes disease. We also know that the elements needed to produce and maintain health—exercise, healthy diet, and a good working environment—are all necessary contributors to an individual's state of balance.

WHAT ARE HERBS?

According to Michael Murray, N.D., the term *herb* refers to a plant-derived compound used for medicinal purposes.[4] *Herb* generally refers to a plant or plant part such as a flower, stem, leaf, root, bark, fruit, seed, or any other plant part used for its medicinal, food flavoring, preservative, or fragrant property. Commonly, any plant or plant part that has been dried, powdered, or formed into an extract or concentrate is considered an herb.[5] Under this definition, any plant used medicinally can be considered an herb, regardless of its safety. For instance, deadly nightshade, a potentially toxic plant, can be considered an herb because it may be used for medicinal purposes.

The expanding field of botanical medicine offers many possibilities for reaping rich rewards. Of an estimated 250,000 to 500,000 plants on the earth today, approximately 5,000 of these plants have been studied for their medicinal properties. In other words, only 1 to 2 percent of all plants on the earth have been investigated as potential medicines! Of that 1 to 2 percent, about 120 plant-derived pharmaceutical medicines and countless numbers of herbs are being sold today on the world market. Let us say that we can find, at the very least, 120 medicines per every 5,000 plants in the world, based on today's numbers. If we studied every plant in the world, research would reveal approximately 12,000 more medicines. Modern medicine, as we know it, would be revolutionized. Since 121 prescription drugs are derived from only ninety species of plants, there is a lot more medicine out there than we know. The cure to the deadliest infectious agent may be hiding somewhere in the rain forest, the mountains, the ocean, or the desert.[6]

BOTANICAL MEDICINE

In twentieth-century America, herbs are not limited to health food stores. Mass-market retailers, mail-order companies, supermarkets, discount warehouses, and pharmacies are among the chief retail distributors of herbal products. But, wait a second . . . did I say that pharmacies sell common everyday herbs? Yes, not only do most pharmacies sell encapsulated herbs, but they also merchandise prescription drugs prepared from plants.

One-fourth of all prescription drugs sold in the United States contain active constituents obtained from plants. Some of the most popular and valuable drugs that have been isolated from plant sources include digoxin, colchicine, yohimbine, codeine, morphine, and vincristine.[7] There are several over-the-counter preparations, too, that use plant compounds. Most people may not realize this because the package may list active botanical components by their Latin names or list one of the active chemical constituents present in the herb. You will be familiar, however, with the brand names since some of the preparations address common symptoms such as constipation (Senokot sold as a laxative) or bad breath (Listerine sold as a breath freshener and antiseptic). They are regularly advertised and enjoy good sales. An estimated $11 billion worth of plant-based medicines are sold in the United States every year and $43 billion worldwide.[8]

The major difference between herbs and drugs, which we will discuss in more depth later in the chapter, is their chemical composition. When naturally derived, pharmaceutical drugs are usually single molecular entities consisting of one isolated, purified chemical.[9] When batches of a prescription drug are produced, they are not expected to vary in structure or quality. Each manufactured tablet will be identical to every other manufactured tablet, ensuring consistency when a particular drug is administered.

In contrast to the single-entity prescription drugs, each herb is a complex composition of many differing constituents. There is no one particular compound totally responsible for its medicinal effects. Thus, scientists and physicians generally recognize herbs for their chemical diversity and variability. While scientists may isolate an active constituent of an herb, there may be thirty other compounds present that work to a lesser degree. Because the so-called active constituent may rely on the workings of other compounds, herbs may need all their constituents to function appropriately. This concept of variability is baffling to orthodox pharmacologists and scientists, but herbalists and naturopathic physicians are well acquainted with this situation.

HERBAL MEDICINE TODAY

The science of herbal medicine has traveled a long way during the past several thousand years. While botanical and conventional medicines still have a long way to go to become fully integrated with each other, the road to cooperation between the two has already started. We are witnessing one of the most significant transformations in health care: a paradigm shift characterized by an increasingly scientific perspective of health that includes more holistic approaches. Physicians, nutritionists, and scientists cannot afford to close their eyes and turn their backs on the overwhelming flood of scientific evidence in support of natural medicine. From one scientific journal to another, new discoveries are being made about natural foods and medicines.

Herbal medicine and other alternative therapies, more accepted in conventional medical circles as of late, are becoming recognized as viable alternatives to orthodox medicine for several reasons. First, they can offer distinctive advantages in dealing with ailments that standard medicine may be ineffective in treating. Second, they often lack the serious side effects so common with many prescription drugs. Third, they tend to support rather than interfere with the body's normal healing process. For these reasons and many more, physicians and patients alike are frequently combining natural and conventional approaches to create a more successful and individualized program of treatment.

In order to explain developments in the field of botanical medicine today, a brief discussion of pharmacognosy, phytochemicals, and nutraceuticals is necessary. You may be familiar with these terms since they are popularly used in many health magazines and in the naturopathic health industry.

Pharmacognosy, the study of natural drugs and their constituents, plays a major role in the development of prescription drugs. If a medicinal compound derived from a plant is strong enough, an interested drug company will seek approval from the United States Food and Drug Administration (FDA) to market the drug. Approval from the FDA is a long and arduous process, to say the least. It takes approximately ten years and $200 million to license a plant-based drug. In addition, the FDA requires the same absolute proof for herbs as it does for new synthetic drugs. This policy is unfair and does not make a whole lot of sense. Because herbs and synthetic drugs differ in their chemical structures and mechanisms of action, they should not be evaluated according to the same guidelines. Thus, herbal remedies are marketed as herbal dietary supplements in the United States, and their manufacturers are generally allowed to make health claims on their behalf.

One of the problems facing the serious research of botanical medicines is the limited patent possibilities. A patent only grants the right to exclude others from making, using, or offering for sale the particular product. By their very nature, most herbal products can not be patented. However, plant chemicals may be successfully synthesized to mimic their natural compounds and thus be awarded a patent. Since plants are not allowed to be patented, there is little incentive for American pharmaceutical companies to perform research on common and widely available herbs.[10]

In contrast, European companies have the incentive to research and develop herbal medicines. Several herbs are classified as drugs in Europe. In Germany, herbs can be marketed as medicines as long as they meet specific guidelines. In fact, the legal requirements for drugs and herbal medicines are the same. Once an herbal medicine is approved for sale, it is sold as an over-the-counter medicine or as a prescription drug based on its application and safety of use. In addition, insurance companies cover herbal products prescribed by a physician.

Most of the recent research done on St. John's wort has been performed in Germany. Currently, the German Commission E, a division of the German Federal Health Authority, equivalent to our FDA, has licensed the sale of St. John's wort for use not only in depression but also for anxiety and nervousness. The German Commission E produces herbal monographs as the basis of herb product regulation and has developed a series of approximately 435 monographs on herbal medicines, each a source of therapeutic as well as clinical information. When herbal products are assessed, the commission relies on several types of data, including research studies, both animal and human, population studies, historical scientific validation of the herb, professional clinical opinions, and patients' opinions. Not every herb is approved; only those that are shown to be safe and sufficiently effective. Dr. Varro E. Tyler, Dean Emeritus of the Purdue University School of Pharmacy and Pharmacal Sciences and a leading expert of medicinal herbs, agrees that the "findings of the German Commission E on herb safety and efficacy constitute the most accurate body of scientific knowledge on that subject available in the world today."[11]

Phytochemicals, or phytonutrients, are "natural plant-based chemicals that have been identified as active compounds in disease prevention."[12] These compounds help regulate vital body processes to maintain health and assist in the fight against disease. Hypericin, one of the active compounds present in St. John's wort is a phytonutrient.

Every plant food contains at least one class of phytochemicals. Examples of different classes include sulfur compounds from onions, garlic, broccoli, and radishes; phenols from fennel, cucumbers, green tea, and grape skins; and fiber from soybeans, flaxseed, apples, and plums. Each one of these phytochemicals is associated with specific immunological actions. For instance, the sulfur compounds are responsible for the promotion of liver enzymes and inhibit cholesterol synthesis. The phenols are reported to aid in the prevention of blood clotting and function as strong antioxidants.

Since scientists began examining the connections between diet and health, a whole new world of potential medicines has opened up. Admittedly, more research is needed to answer specific questions about the number of different phytochemicals necessary for a balanced diet or the causes of nutritional deficiencies. As the investigation of phytochemicals continues, we will undoubtedly be provided with more information in the future.

Nutraceutical is an umbrella term encompassing any active, natural components obtained from plant or animal sources. Thus, phytochemicals, obtained strictly from plant sources, are a class of nutraceuticals. The compounds in St. John's wort, therefore, may be referred to as phytochemicals, phytonutrients, or nutraceuticals.

WHEN HERBS DON'T WORK

As I mentioned earlier, herbs are complex combinations of many different ingredients. These ingredients work together to produce a physical effect on the body, but in order for an herb to be effective, the active ingredients must exist at certain potencies. Many factors influence the quality of an herb, including the condition of the soil, the environment, climate, farming methods (i.e., organic or inorganic), and preparation methods. Each factor is essential to creating a quality herb product. If any one of these factors, or a multitude of them, is compromised, then the herb's effectiveness may be reduced.

In the past, one of the drawbacks to using botanical medicines was the relative inconsistency between batches of herbs. Let me illustrate this point through an example. Imagine two people walking into a health food store to buy bilberry *(Vaccinium myrtillus)*, an herb indicated in the treatment of weak eyesight. Jane selects a bottle of bilberry capsules marketed by company X, and Bob buys one marketed by company Y. Since bilberry may be grown in different parts of the world, it is likely that the companies supplying the bilberry purchased it from different manufacturers, who in turn purchased the herb from different farmers. The quality of bilberry produced will vary due to soil conditions and other factors discussed above. While company X's bilberry product works for Jane, company Y's bilberry product fails to work for Bob, who may conclude that bilberry is ineffective as a botanical medicine.

In this scenario, it is easy to blame bilberry and label it as ineffective. If we buy an herbal product that fails to work, we may feel justified in calling the herb worthless, but it may be the soil, the cold air, or the product's age that is responsible for its ineffectiveness—or, it may be company Y's failure to produce a good product.

The scenario becomes even more complicated when each bottle of bilberry capsules produced by company X and Y may differ from batch to batch. Therefore, when Jane returns to the health food store and purchases the same brand of capsules, this time, the herb fails to produce any results. She may assume that the herb never worked in the first place and that any perceived results were due to the placebo effect. Finally, both persons are unhappy with the herbs they paid for, and they have good reason to be. Nobody wants to purchase a medicine whose consistency varies from batch to batch.

STANDARDIZED HERBS

Standardized herbs now give us greater control over manipulating the power of herbs. Standardized extracts ensure that the potency of the active ingredients of an herb—those believed to give the herb its therapeutic benefits—are consistent in every dose. This means that from batch to batch, the range level of active ingredients will be consistent.

Exactly what is standardized in each herb depends on the herb. Some of the ingredients standardized in an herb are the ones considered more biologically active than the other constituents. Other standardized compounds are "marker" compounds, chemicals that are simply unique to the plant.[13] Hence, a standardized compound can consist of one ingredient or a group of ingredients.

Most companies that sell standardized herbs blend the standardized extract with the whole herb for a combined effect. This way, the other lesser known compounds that may be responsible for any of the health benefits are included. Sometimes, however, the standardized extract is sold alone. Most naturopaths and people in the health food industry disagree with the manufacturing of isolated active ingredients for several reasons. First, the isolated constituent is sometimes less active biologically than the crude herb. In contrast to those in the United States, researchers in Europe are fully aware that isolated plant drugs do not always have the greatest therapeutic effect.[14] Second, the isolation and modification of an active compound may be dangerous. Evidence of this comes from the pharmaceutical companies that first isolated and marketed the alkaloid ephedrine from the Chinese herb ma huang *(Ephedra sinica)* as a treatment for asthma. It soon became clear that the drug had the insidious side effect of raising blood pressure to dangerously high levels. Interestingly, there are six other related alkaloids in the herb, one of which lowers blood pressure.[15] It seems that some compounds balance the action of others.

One of the arguments against standardization is a holistic one. Some herbalists contend that standardization upsets the natural balance of the herb. Once the balance is upset, it can never be achieved again. Although the standardized extract is mixed with the other, so-called inactive ingredients, opponents argue that the result is nothing more than a druglike medicine masking itself as a natural botanical medicine.

This argument seems like a strong one on the surface, but it does not hold a lot of weight. First, standardization has played an important role in advancing the acceptance of herbal medicine. Throughout numerous clinical studies, standardized botanical medicines have been proven to be effective in the treatment of numerous disorders. Because of the variability of plant compounds based on soil, harvesting and preparation methods, and so on, standardization ensures a measurable, specific range of active ingredients. Otherwise, scientific trials will be inconclusive and consumers will not know what they are buying. In addition, the pharmalogical activity of a plant can actually be enhanced by standardization: the level of active ingredients can be increased while the potentially unsafe compounds can be decreased.[16]

Of course, we are most concerned with St. John's wort. The clinical studies of St. John's wort used a standardized extract, and you will want to purchase the standardized version since it has been shown to be the most effective.

SCIENTIFIC TIMES, SCIENTIFIC COMPANIES

The health food industry is now an intensely competitive market in which herb companies are vying for a slice of the money pie. In the effort to do so, they are offering better quality service than was previously provided. More attention has been focused on key issues of quality, potency, and purity. Too often, these issues have been overlooked in the race to catch the customer's dollar and fatten the businessperson's pocket. So while the competition for business has become stiff, the result is better botanical preparations for the customer.

If herbal preparations are to become more scientific, then so must the companies that prepare them. The use of high-tech systems to determine batch-to-batch consistency of herbs is now becoming the norm at many herb companies. Careful analysis is made of all the incoming materials, and if a batch fails to meet the quality control standards established, it is returned or rejected. The development of an in-house laboratory is no longer an idea on paper but now something almost required by companies.[17] Intense scrutiny and laboratory examination are expected of industry leaders.

The leaders of the industry have taken further steps to ensure the quality and integrity of herbal products available today. Some companies support nutritional research studies at various medical institutions across the country. Others prepare their herbs in FDA-approved facilities. It is not uncommon for experts in the field of nutrition, such as nutritional biochemists and medical doctors, to sit on the board to help oversee product development. Many companies even invite customers to their facilities for tours and an inside peek at daily operations. As science progresses, so do the companies that formulate and produce the herbs.

The business of herbs does not appear to be going away any time soon. Every year more and more people are becoming interested in herbal medicine, and every year the herb market continues to grow. As long as the bridge exists between traditional herbal medicine and modern pharmaceutical techniques, the market for natural medicine will expand. Certainly, if the past success of the health food market is a good indicator of its future, we have reason to suspect that herbs will be around for a long time.

CHAPTER 3

UNDERSTANDING DEPRESSION

As if a phantom caress'd me,
I thought I was not alone walking here by the shore;
But the one I thought was with me as now I walk by the
shore, the one I loved that caress'd me,
As I lean and look through the glimmering light, that one
has utterly disappear'd,
And those appear that are hateful to me and mock me.

Walt Whitman
"As if a Phantom Caress'd Me"

At one time or another, everyone experiences a case of the "blues"—the unpleasant feeling that everything is wrong. Sometimes the condition has no apparent precipitating event and disappears as quickly as it came. A bad date, horrible conversation, or argument with your friend may cause enough distress to upset you for several days. Other times, the feelings may result from another problem such as a bout of cold or flu or a hormonal imbalance. In general, the brief stresses and strains of daily living do not require medical treatment. Within a couple of weeks the blues clear up, and you feel like yourself again.

But what happens when the blues stay? Unlike a period of grief that passes in a couple of hours or days, depression lingers and persists. Occasional feelings of sadness are a normal part of daily living, although people may refer them to as "depression." However, "real" depression is a different matter and more than a brief down-and-out feeling.

The word *depression* has become so overused that its clinical meaning has become obscured. It is quite common to refer to anything unpleasant as depressing; the meaning of the word has become all-inclusive. People use the word *depressed* when they might once have described themselves as feeling dejected, unsatisfied, or grief stricken. But, depression is characterized by persistent discouragement and hopelessness. Despair is central to the condition, the feeling that nothing will change and there is nothing to look forward to.

"Perhaps the simplest definition of depression is, as Harvard Medical School psychiatrist Ned Gassem said, 'misery requiring treatment.'"[1] Depressed people not only feel bad, they feel incredibly miserable. They lose interest in favorite activities, friends, and sex, or any other form of pleasure. They experience drops in energy but ironically have trouble sleeping. They may think something is physically wrong with them, but they fail to respond to medical treatment. Disturbing thoughts and feelings persist and become increasingly debilitating. Excessive worrying may accompany the feeling of despair. Often, the act of suicide is considered.

According to the National Institute of Mental Health, symptoms of depression can include:

- Persistent sad, anxious, or "empty" mood
- Feelings of hopelessness, pessimism
- Feelings of guilt, worthlessness, helplessness
- Loss of interest or pleasure in hobbies and activities that were once enjoyed, including sex
- Insomnia, early-morning awakening, or oversleeping
- Appetite and/or weight loss or overeating and weight gain
- Decreased energy, fatigue, feeling "slowed down"
- Thoughts of death or suicide; suicide attempts
- Restlessness, irritability
- Difficulty concentrating, remembering, making decisions
- Persistent physical symptoms that do not respond to treatment, such as headaches, digestive disorders, and chronic pain

In the workplace, depression often may be recognized by:

- Decreased productivity
- Morale problems

- Lack of cooperation
- Safety problems, accidents
- Absenteeism
- Frequent complaints of being tired all the time
- Complaints of unexplained aches and pains
- Alcohol and drug abuse

Most people have experienced one or more of these symptoms at some time in their lives. We all get "depressed" at times. You may lose your appetite, feel "out of it" for several days, and have a hard time sleeping. But, that does not mean that you are clinically depressed. So, before you assume that you have a major depressive disorder, compare what you are feeling with the intensity of the symptoms of clinical depression. Perhaps what you are feeling is perfectly normal. In which case, you may justifiably ask yourself at what point do "passing blue moods" become clinical depression?

Sad or Depressed?

According to the American Psychiatric Association's Diagnostic and Statistical Manual of Mental Disorders (DSM IV), the symptoms of major depressive disorder (also referred to as clinical depression) last at least two weeks and may persist for years. Not all of the symptoms mentioned above occur in each individual who becomes depressed. Some people experience few symptoms while others experience many, but in order to qualify as major depressive disorder, at least the first or second symptom must be present along with at least four other symptoms during the two-week time frame.

And the condition does not include the normal reaction to a traumatic event as in the death of a loved one. While the grief process may include similar symptoms, it should not be confused with or classified as a major depressive disorder unless grieving persists for an extended period of time and meets the first two symptoms. Sometimes the normal grief process does not include absolute hopelessness and despair, essential symptoms of clinical depression. Unremitting grief certainly may develop into pathological depression, but it should not be classified as such initially. Depression lasts, on the average, a period of three to eight months. Since it lasts longer than temporary feelings of despondency, sadness, and lethargy, it injuriously affects day-to-day functioning in a negative way.[2]

Unfortunately, no definitive hormonal or blood tests can diagnose depression at this time. However, blood tests are currently being developed and perhaps someday many people will benefit from a more conclusive means of diagnosing this complex and often misunderstood illness. In the meantime, doctors must rely on a variety of other observations to make a clinical diagnosis.

Mental health professionals rely on recognizing the familiar pattern of symptoms of depression in their diagnosis, even though a few of the symptoms may be absent from the pattern in a particular case. Biologically and psychologically, every person is different—born with a unique set of genes and brain circuits that influence the symptoms of depression in a variety of ways. One person may express sadness, for example, by crying; another may express sadness through silence. Different people experience the same mental illness in different ways.[3]

Some depressed people may find themselves becoming excessively irritated with trifling matters and more vulnerable to sudden outbursts of rage. Their patience with others may wear thin and a general feeling of annoyance and hostility may take over their character.

Other depressives may manifest their symptoms in an entirely opposite manner. They may continuously sigh and mope around, occasionally bursting into tears for no apparent reason. Sometimes they may alternate between elation and depression. One moment the depressive is smiling and perhaps talking about how wonderful life is, but the next moment the depressive is crying and cursing his or her very existence. Someone observing this behavior can find it very difficult to discern what is going on in the depressive's mind.

Depressives tend to be extremely sensitive to others' statements. A few kind words may temporarily lift their spirits until a harsh response sends them back into despair. For this reason, people should be very careful with what they say around depressives. A teacher's gentle criticism may unknowingly drive a depressed student further into his or her sadness, or a couple of words from a well-meaning spouse might be misinterpreted and have a devastating effect on the depressive. Depressives have difficulty processing criticism objectively; instead they concentrate only on the bad, failing to hear the good.

Depression obviously influences the way one relates to other people.

Some depressives hide away from the world, locking themselves up in their rooms and refusing to go out or to answer the phone. (The American poet Emily Dickinson provides a famous example of this reclusive behavior.) After struggling to manage a normal nine-to-five job, reclusive depressives crave being alone, away from the world. Finding social ties meaningless, they destroy any sense of a social life, often cutting their ties with family members and friends.

Other depressives need people in order to establish a sense of security. Instead of locking themselves in the house, they are constantly searching for a crowd. They are especially keen on finding someone willing to give them a forum where they can discuss their problems freely. The depressive may continue talking on and on without ever showing any interest in the other person. They may make excessive demands on peoples' time, unconsciously enjoying projecting their misery onto others.

People who suffer from clinical depression are not necessarily aware of the seriousness of their condition. When they experience a prolonged period of grief, they may think they are reacting to the situation in a healthy way and may not recognize the mood as depressive. They may assume that low moods are a normal part of day-to-day living and believe there is no disease present or treatment available. This is especially true of people who experience any of the symptoms of depression intermittently or at low levels over a long period of time.

Since depression has such a detrimental effect on functional living, evaluating and treating oneself for the condition can be difficult. This is why people who think they might be suffering from clinical depression should seek diagnosis and treatment from a professional. Depression can continue indefinitely if not properly treated, and unlike a severe bout with measles or chicken pox, a bout with depression does not confer lifelong immunity. Disabling episodes of depression may occur more than once in a lifetime.

TYPES OF DEPRESSION

Professionals in the mental health field classify depression as a mood disorder that affects a person's thoughts and feelings. Depressive disorders come in different forms, and I will touch on the three most prevalent. All fall under the category of primary depression: major depression, dysthymia, and bipolar disorder (formally called manic-depressive illness).

Each of these forms manifests itself differently in every individual according to variations in the number of symptoms, their severity, and persistence. St. John's wort has been shown to be effective in the treatment of mild to moderate depression.

Major depression is characterized by significant depressive episodes. As previously described, these episodes include depressed mood for at least a two-week period in addition to the exhibition of several of the other symptoms listed by the National Institute of Mental Health. Without treatment, a major depressive episode may last anywhere between six months and two years. In order to be classified as major depression, the illness cannot result from a general medical condition, substance abuse, or schizophrenia.[4]

The second type of depression is called dysthymia or dysthymic disorder (formerly referred to as neurotic depression). Dysthymia is best described as prolonged sadness. The depressed mood exists for a minimum of two weeks and is accompanied by some of the usual symptoms of depression: poor appetite or overeating, sleeping too little or too much, low energy or fatigue, low self-esteem, poor concentration, and feelings of hopelessness. The symptoms of dysthymia are less severe than those of major depression.

James McCullough, Ph.D., director of the Unipolar Mood Disorders Institute at Virginia Commonwealth University, in Richmond, Virginia, compares dysthymia to "a low-grade infection people just can't get rid of. They're not taken out of the work force or the home—they just feel bad most of the time."[5] A chronic mild depression follows the sufferer wherever he or she goes. The person might not realize he or she is sick but instead figures that life is intensely difficult all of the time. Consequently, the person does not experience life and the emotions at a normally healthy level.

This form of depression is one of the most difficult to diagnose and manage. Sometimes sufferers of dysthymia can develop major depression simultaneously and experience what is sometimes called double depression, a combination that can be particularly serious and hard to treat. Further, persons suffering from double depression are at a higher risk of recurrence. The treatment for this disorder, though, is the same as that for major depression: psychotherapy, drug therapy, or a combination of both.

The final form of depression, considered the most dramatic mood disorder, is bipolar illness. Major depression and dysthymia are forms of unipolar depression. Bipolar disorder involves rapidly alternating episodes of extreme sadness and elation. A manic episode is characterized by a decreased need for sleep, inflated self-esteem, high energy, racing thoughts, and a tendency toward irritability and anger. While manic attacks may come and go quickly, episodes of depression are slower to develop and disappear. The first manic episode usually develops in a person's twenties, and in most cases, before age thirty-five. A manic episode is more likely to occur after major life stresses, such as divorce, or as the side effect of one of the standard antidepressant drugs. A major depressive episode usually trails a manic one. Unfortunately, bipolar illness does not follow any simple formula. There is much variation in the disorder, which is measured by the frequencies of alternating mania and depression, and the time periods in between these highs and lows. Examples of famous people who may have had bipolar illness include Ernest Hemingway, Virginia Woolf, Vincent Van Gogh, and quite possibly, Mark Twain.

CAUSES OF DEPRESSION

The exact mechanism, or mechanisms, through which depression occurs has not yet been identified. Most of the time, a combination of factors is responsible: increased stresses, physical illness, environmental and social factors, and significant trauma. Sometimes depression appears to be hereditary, passed from one person to another in the family genes. Other times, it can be the result of a chemical imbalance in the brain.

You are, no doubt, familiar with the debate between nature and nurture. Some believe that human emotions and ailments are influenced solely by biology, while others are intent on explaining human emotions and ailments as a consequence of life experiences. One of today's hottest topics, the nature versus nurture debate turns up everywhere: appearing in newspaper and magazine headlines, in the movies, and on the television.

Fueled by the nature-nurture debate, scientists and psychologists are asking if behavioral conditions or biological ailments are the result of genetic destiny or of one's psychological processes? If they are biologically based, then people need not take responsibility for their diseases.

A belief in genetic legacy denies individual will and responsibility—if disease is genetic, there is nothing anyone can do about it. Thus, those suffering from depression may view themselves as victims of biology and not as agents capable of choosing their emotional futures.

On the other hand, if the condition results from one's way of thinking or one's environment, perhaps all that may be required of the depressive is a willful personal decision to feel better. If that does not work, the environment can also be changed. Yet some sufferers of depression who would like to believe that depression is solely a matter of choice cannot seem to "snap out of it." There must be more involved than simply psychology alone.

IT IS IN THE BIOLOGY

Every week we hear about a new gene discovered for one trait or another, and biological determinism enjoys popular support among some of the largest medical bodies today. The National Institute of Mental Health is a government agency that supports and conducts research to improve the diagnosis, treatment, and prevention of mental illness. Two decades ago the agency concentrated on social psychiatry, a branch of psychiatry dedicated to assisting the mentally ill by eliminating certain social injustices such as racism and poverty. Today, however, the institute has largely changed its focus and almost exclusively concentrates on brain research and the genetic factors of emotional diseases.[6]

Major advances in neuroscience have opened up a world of information that was not available fifty years ago. Researchers have successfully identified gene mutations and their relevant effects on emotions, and science may have replaced Sigmund Freud's psychological theories. Years ago depression was interpreted as the result of psychological trauma. Today, according to Donna Hales, author of *Depression*, "Researchers have identified genetic markers for manic depression on different chromosomes (the rodlike structures within each cell that contain genetic instructions)."[7] This new evidence suggests that the depression may be something waiting to happen, occurring "coincidentally" after a precipitating event, such as the death of a loved one. The brain is no longer the mystery that has defied explanation for thousands of years but an intricate system of chemistry and connections that are currently being discovered.

Most psychiatrists comfortably define depression as an illness, a brain disorder with genetic roots. The illness is thought of as a disruption of normal connections in the brain. The brain's transmitters of information function like a network of interdependent computers. When one computer misfires, the connections between all the computers crash.

BRAIN CHEMISTRY

The activities of nerve cells in the brain depend on a system of complex reactions and movements of molecules. If none of these chemical reactions or molecular movements existed, then emotions and behavior probably could not exist either. Thought processes are the end result of the molecular activities carried out by nerve cells in the brain.[8] Although alternative theories exist, the chemical/biological model forms the foundation for the current progress neuroscience has made in comprehending the brain.

Brain chemistry changes according to behavior. Drugs are not the only substances capable of producing those chemical changes. Ordinary everyday experiences can induce variations in brain chemistry. The most mundane human actions, such as falling asleep or making lunch, are responsible for complex chemical reactions in the brain. Chemical reactions prompt us to get up early in the morning or inspire us to eat something cold or to exercise. If one takes a drive through the rolling hills of the Baja California peninsula, stares at the sunset over the great Pacific Ocean, and gasps in awe of the beauty of nature, one feels amazement because "the scene initiates chemical reactions in one's brain."[9] The brain is believed to be the seat of mental chemistry.

This belief is the basis of the "biological revolution" in psychiatry, which contends that a person develops a mental illness when the brain's chemical interactions change enough to cause the brain to malfunction. Because psychiatrists now label mental illness as an organic disease caused by a defective brain function, drugs are offered as a form of treatment to modify existing brain chemistry, allowing the person to experience health once again.[10]

Of course, more must be learned about brain activity and about how drugs influence it. The view of mental illness as a predominantly organic disease is the most widely accepted viewpoint among doctors, especially since standard antidepressants like Prozac and Paxil seem to work succesfully. Proponents of neuroscience believe that brain chemistry can be altered for the better and that chemical treatment is an efficacious cure for mental illness.

A BIOCHEMICAL FACTORY

In order to explain how brain chemistry relates to depression and St. John's wort, let me introduce the three most crucial neurotransmitters, or chemicals, that allow the brain cells (neurons) to communicate with one another: norepinephrine, serotonin, and dopamine. Scientists postulate that neurons in the brain communicate with each other by sending amino acid molecules, or neurotransmitters, across the synapse, or space between the cells, to the receptors on the other side. In other words, one nerve cell talks to another using messengers. When neurotransmitters are at abnormally low levels, messages cannot get across the gaps and fail to reach their destinations. Scientists think that depression is related to a lack of biological amines—lower than normal levels of norepinephrine, serotonin, and dopamine—or to the neurotransmitters' failure to properly fit their receptors.

Scientists are unsure which of the two biochemical theories more accurately depicts the predominant cause of depression. There is lack of evidence to consistently support the claim that depression results from too little serotonin or norepinephrine. Although drug-induced increases in neurotransmitter levels have resulted in mood-elevating effects for many depressed people, several limitations and inconsistencies in this theory have been cited, the most prominent being the several weeks lag time between the biochemical effect of the drug and signs of clinical improvement. Even though the levels of serotonin and norepinephrine increase soon after the drug is taken, the clinical antidepressant effect may not appear for at least two weeks. Because of this, new explanations for the biological amine theory became necessary.

The biological amine theory has been refined and focus has moved from the synapses to the receptors. In a process known as reuptake— once the neurotransmitters lock into receptors on target cells, following the neuron's initial release—the neurotransmitter is taken back in. It is thought that the postsynaptic receptors may be hyperresponsive due to the lack of available neurotransmitters in the synapse. Thus, when a drug blocks the neurotransmitter reuptake, the presynaptic activity normalizes (normal amounts of the specified neurotransmitter become available at the receptor) and postsynaptic receptors down-regulate to a normal level of responsiveness.[11]

Scientists believe that a lack of serotonin, one of the three primary neurotransmitters, may be responsible for depression. The human nervous system retains at least fourteen classes of serotonin receptors, each fitted to a particular section of the amine. Because different types of brain cells house unlike receptors, those responses to serotonin vary greatly. When the brain is low on serotonin, a person may be affected by a number of symptoms often suffered by depressed persons such as anxiety, confused thinking, disturbance of the sleep cycle, irritability, and abnormal appetite. Serotonergic antidepressants such as Prozac, Zoloft, or Paxil may be prescribed because they manipulate serotonin levels by enhancing the amount of available serotonin in the synaptic gap between the nerve cells. The efficacy of drugs like Prozac proves that when depression occurs, serotonin plays a major role.

While serotonin is one of the chemicals in the brain that transfers messages from one cell to the next, another one hundred–some-odd chemicals are involved in brain activity. These include gamma-aminobutyric acid (GABA), and norepinephrine and dopamine, both mentioned earlier. Evidence suggests that the neurotransmitters affect one another, and that serotonin probably interacts with other brain chemicals, but scientists are not quite sure how or to what degree serotonin is involved.

While the symptoms of depression may be similar among certain sufferers, the chemical abnormalities that underlie the symptoms can be different. When a psychiatrist diagnoses depression and prescribes a psychiatric drug for its treatment, the doctor believes the illness result from a change or imbalance in brain chemistry due to genetic or biochemical causes. Whether such brain chemistry is due to biological or psychological causes, or some combination of both, the efficacy of medication suggests that, whatever the source, depression involves neurotransmitters and neurons.

PRESCRIPTION ANTIDEPRESSANTS

Antidepressants are medications used to treat depression. Like any other drug, they are used to correct or compensate for some bodily malfunction. Antidepressants fall into three major categories: monoamine oxidase inhibitors (MAOIs), tricyclics (TCAs), and selective serotonin reuptake inhibitors (SSRIs). Each of these antidepressant types is still actively used today in combating depression. As with other psychotherapeutic medications, different antidepressants do not always produce the same positive, mood-elevating effect for everyone.

MAOIs

The MAOIs are one of the first two classes of drugs used initially in the treatment of depression. It was first discovered—accidently—in the 1950s. Originally a drug used to treat tuberculosis, MAOIs were found effective in unexpectedly elevating the mood of tuberculosis patients. In 1957 scientists discovered that MAOIs were helpful in the treatment of depressive disorders in psychiatric patients.

Monoamine oxidase is an enzyme found throughout the body that is responsible for the breakdown of the neurotransmitters such as norepinephrine, serotonin, and dopamine. This action by MAO inhibitors limits the activity of monoamine oxidase, preventing it from destroying those important biological amines. As a result, the amounts of the specific neurotransmitters are increased and normal mood states are restored. MAOIs are commonly used in the treatment of major depression, especially atypical depression and bipolar disorder. Examples of MAOIs on the pharmaceutical market include Nardil and Parnate.

The main side effects associated with the use of MAOIs include constipation, fatigue, headache, low blood pressure, sexual difficulties, sedation, and rapid heartbeat. A disadvantage of taking MAOIs is that they react with certain foods and beverages containing a substance called tyramine. Normally, tyramine is broken down in the intestine before it is absorbed, when MAOIs prevent the breakdown from occurring, tyramine may enter the bloodstream where it can have serious, even fatal, side effects. These include a dangerous rise in blood pressure, possible seizure, or coma. Among a long list of dietary restrictions for patients taking MAOIs are the avoidance of beer, aged meats and cheeses, wine, and over-the-counter cold medications. Because the potential of serious side effects does exist, MAOIs are usually recommended to persons who do not respond to the other classes of drugs, and they are used principally in the treatment of persons affected by major depressive illness.

TCAs

The tricyclic antidepressants were introduced at roughly the same time as the MAOIs. In 1956, Roland Kuhn, a Swiss psychiatrist, while studying imipramine (now commonly referred to as Tofranil) for its antipsychotic effects, noticed an unexpected mood-enhancing effect in those taking the drug—thus the first tricyclic was discovered.

The name *tricyclic* refers to the chemical structure of the drug—a triple carbon ring chemical structure. They are thought to work by decreasing the rate of reuptake, or reabsorption, of the neurotransmitters serotonin and norepinephrine by nerve cells. A norepinephrine imbalance, that amine responsible for regulating arousal and alterness, is thought to contribute to depressed moods and fatigure. The success of the TCAs with depression has led to their use in treating other disorders, including chronic pain, bulimia, panic attacks, and migraine. Some names of drugs in this category are quite recognizable: Tofranil, Elavil, and Anafranil.

Because TCAs block neurotransmitters other than serotonin and norepinephrine, they produce a list of burdensome side effects. These side effects vary according to the specific medication and the individual. For example, of all the tricyclic drugs, Elavil has the greatest sedative effect, leaving patients extremely tired and groggy. Other side effects of the cyclic drugs include dry mouth, confusion, muscle twitches, urinary retention, lowered blood pressure, increased pulse, and blurred vision. The TCAs can potentially cause serious cardiac complications; therefore, doctors must take a careful cardiac history of the patient.

While these drugs continue to play a role in the treatment of depression, for the most part they have been replaced by the newer depression medicines, the SSRIs. The latter are said to be more effective for treatment and have fewer and milder side effects.

SSRIs

Heralded as breakthrough drugs, selective serotonin reuptake inhibitors (SSRIs), particularly Prozac, attained celebrity status shortly after their release in the United States in 1988. Prozac, Paxil, and Zoloft were widely acclaimed because they treated depression without the adverse effects of the TCAs and did not necessitate a change in diet. The SSRIs work by potentiating serotonin neurotransmission by inhibiting the brain cells' reuptake of the vital neurotransmitter. Unlike the TCAs, which worked with norepinephrine and to a lesser extent serotonin, the success of the SSRIs is attributed strictly to its serotonin potentiating and receptor desensitizing effects.

It seems as if serotonin has a more stabilizing effect on specific mental ailments than do the neurotransmitters altered by other medications. Ailments other than depression for which SSRIs are reported to have success in treating include obsessive-compulsive disorder, panic disorder, bulimia, schizophrenia, and alcoholism. SSRIs, however, are not free of side effects—they include nervousness, anxiety, sexual dysfunction, gastrointestinal distress, and insomnia.

SSRIs have replaced TCAs as the first choice for prescription antidepressants. They are often prescribed to elderly persons with cardiovascular illness, and are recommended as an adjunct to estrogen replacement therapy.

Prozac

The popularity of Prozac follows the typical celebrity drug's life: First proclaimed the wonder drug of the century, appearing in newspaper headlines across the globe, and touted as a safe, effective cure-all for psychological conditions ranging from mood swings to speaker's anxiety to premenstrual syndrome. Its remarkable influence over serotonin yielded much greater success than the TCAs and it soon became the first choice in treatment for many psychological disorders. Furthermore, its effectiveness on serotonin levels, coupled with comparably mild side effects to the earlier generations of antidepressants, earmarked it for greatness. Peter Breggin wrote a runaway bestseller, *Listening to Prozac*, that discussed the intricacies of treatment with Prozac and its remarkable success in treating and resolving a broad spectrum of psychiatric disorders previously thought to require psychotherapy. The successful results of Prozac treatment helped confirm the perspective of mental illness as biological in nature. In a sense, Prozac treatment seemed a stunning victory over psychotherapy because with it people found immediate and successful treatment for their mental illness.

The drug also became the target of attacks by the Church of Scientology whose ultimate goal became removing the drug from the marketplace. The Church was bothered by Prozac's biological magic bullet approach to depression, feeling that it dangerously absolved the individual from any personal responsibility for his ailment; that the ailment had not been treated, but simply covered up by the antidepressant; and that Scientologists, according to a report aired in 1991 on CBS's *Sixty Minutes*, wanted Scientology to replace Prozac as the world's foremost mental-health therapy. But Prozac soon came under heavy attack, and it even was alleged to be responsible for promoting suicidal and violent tendencies in some individuals. A man in Lousiville, Kentucky, who gunned down eight coworkers before killing himself, was found to be on Prozac. A similar incident occurred at a restaurant in San Ysidro, California, in which a man ruthlessy gunned down customers. Later, he was found to be on Prozac, as well.

Doctor Martin Teicher, a Harvard Psychiatrist, prescribed Prozac for several of his patients, after which each began to experience suicidal thoughts. When he took them off the drug, the suicidal thoughts disappeared. In 1990 he published his findings in the *American Journal of Psychiatry*, adding fuel to the growing controversy surrounding Prozac. The drug's life on the market was threatened, but in a decision backed by the National Mental Health Institute and the American Psychiatric Association the FDA reaffirmed Prozac's safety. Now, after a long hard road, Prozac is once again accepted among physicians and patients alike.

WHICH DRUG SHOULD BE USED FIRST?

Choosing the correct drug can be a matter of trial and error. According to the National Foundation for Depressive Illness, even when depression is correctly diagnosed, tranquilizers and sleeping pills are prescribed twice as often as the right antidepressant.[12] A drug may be effective for one person, but not for another, and because the chemical abnormality, the relative cause of the disease, is largely unknown, an effective treatment can be difficult to determine.

Patients with the same mental illness respond differently to different drugs. Often patients must try several drugs before they find a medication that proves effective. The effectiveness of the drug, however, may be compromised by its annoying, and sometimes dangerous side effects— a concern of many who are currently taking antidepressants or contemplating their use. About 30 percent of patients taking standard drugs for depression, including Prozac, experience decreased sexual desire, difficulty in reaching orgasm, and potency problems. As one might expect, this is a great deterrent to experimenting with standard antidepressants.

MAO inhibitors, a separate class of antidepressant drugs, can have especially serious side effects that include possible drug-induced hepatitis with jaundice, nervousness, and low white blood cell count (possible side effects of Nardil).[13] While some people find a way to live comfortably with the side effects, others must find a substitute medication. Still others quit the drugs and search for benign alternatives such as St. John's wort.

A pharmacological cocktail—a combination of various drugs that effectively treat depressive symtoms—may also be an option in drug treatment. Dosage is also a factor in the administration of medicine. Physicians must decide on a therapeutic dose that will prove effective without over- or undermedicating the patient. Furthermore, the relief provided by the drug usually ends when the drug taking stops. It does not continue past the last dose, and does not prevent the patient from suffering a relapse in the future.

For many people psychiatric drugs are clearly not the preferred method of treatment for depression. Psychotherapy is another option; in some cases it may be successfully integrated with the administration of psychiatric drugs.

IT'S ALL IN YOUR MIND

Some researchers still maintain that depression is primarily psychological in nature, a view largely recognized as Freudian in that Sigmund Freud was one of the first to psychologize the mind. According to Freud, early life experiences influence our future emotional state of being. For instance, if a child's father dies, the child may repress her grief and then as an adult become severely depressed and emotionally dependent on other people. Each deprivation a child experiences increases the risk that depression will occur in adulthood.

There are several forms of psychotherapy available—cognitive, behavioral, and interpersonal. Each type has been clinically evaluated and tested and all three appear to be effective. Cognitive therapy teaches patients to identify and change negative thought patterns through changing interpretations of actions or events. Behavioral therapy focuses on specific behaviors such as shyness or obsessiveness and attempts to rectify them. Interpersonal therapy targets relationships in the individual's life and concentrates on tactics for improving them.

Dr. Aaron Beck pioneered a form of verbal treatment called cognitive therapy, which attributes depression to faulty thinking patterns. Dr. Beck states that "depression is caused by negative views of the self, the environment, and the future which have been learned during childhood and adolescence." He advocates a treatment that teaches depressives how to identify negative thinking patterns and then to reverse them.[14] In the cognitive view of depression, distorted or irrational ideas contribute to the onset of the disease and thus patients play a large role in changing their own thinking patterns, thus ultimately treating their own depression.

Plenty of evidence supports the effectiveness of behavioral modification. Even with medication, depression and mental illness are often very difficult to treat and cure, and many people will need some form of psychotherapy. Prominent psychiatrists such as Dr. William S. Appleton advocate the view that psychotherapy has the potential to alter brain chemistry in the same way that watching the sunset induces positive chemical reactions in the brain.

Medication is typically more effective for the physiological aspects of depression such as low energy, poor appetite, and insomnia; psychotherapy has more of an effect on the psychological components of depression such as guilt, despair, and low self-esteem. Among the most common psychological problems that can increase the risk of depression are divorce, retirement, sexual difficulties, money problems, social problems, and death of a friend or relative. As mentioned earlier, while experiencing grief after a traumatic life event is normal, it can be unhealthy if the grief turns into major depression. Counseling can help people gain insight into change, resolve unproductive thinking patterns, and provide practical advice and reassurance. It may even initiate chemical reactions that decrease symptoms of depression and prevent its recurrence. Patients who have undergone psychotherapy, particularly cognitive therapy, relapse into depression at a much lower rate than those who have been treated with antidepressants alone.

PSYCHOBIOLOGY: A MORE HOLISTIC VIEW

After exploring the complicated interplay between biology and psychology, researchers feel it is impossible to choose one as more important than the other. In fact, the either/or approach—meaning it either has to be "talk" therapy or "neurotransmitter" therapy—is an outdated way of viewing mental illness. People are made up of a combination of elements that cannot be explained by chemistry alone. Additional scientific evidence is directing us to a more complete perspective on illness that includes biological, psychological, and environmental factors. In *Medication of the Mind*, Dr. Richard Restak of George Washington University writes, "Our mind and brain are like two sides of one coin: if we look at the coin from one side, it appears to be all biology; turn the coin over, and we encounter the subjective world of thoughts and dreams and images that comprise the human mind. To that extent we are hybrid creatures—not entirely servants of biology, yet not entirely independent of the influences imposed upon us by the structure and function of our brain."[15]

Molecular reactions do not explain everything about how the mind responds to and recovers from depression. Moving away from a strict biological model of mental illness, understanding one's basic character and personality is an important part of treatment. Psychiatrist Keith Russel Ablow tells his depressed patients that they have the capacity to take a pro-active response to their mental illness, believing that although depression may have a biological component, weakness of character allows mental illness to proliferate. By understanding that they are not forever locked into a mode of mental suffering and that they have choice and responsibility, depressed patients can help cure themselves of their illness.[16]

Thanks to advances in ongoing genetic research, the oversimplified Mendelian model of genetics in which single genes determine our fate—one gene creates a manic depression and another leads to alcoholism—is quickly becoming obsolete. In contrast to the old idea that they were stagnant and nonchanging, genes are believed to be dynamic entities. Human behaviors involve many different genes that are controlled by internal and external forces ranging from the things we lump under nature (viruses and birth complications) to those we lump under nurture (parents and diet).

Potentially, each one of us may carry genes that predispose us to multiple mood disorders, but having these genes does not necessarily lead to possessing certain traits. A gene may express its trait under certain conditions and in certain environments, so ultimately environment may be just as integral to the formation of a human being as are the genes. Nature and nurture intertwined.

SEEKING TREATMENT

The ultimate challenge for anyone suffering from depression is to find proper treatment. Should one try psychiatric drugs, psychotherapy, or a combination of both?

Certain types of depression respond better to certain therapeutic approaches. Chemical treatment is especially effective for biogenic psychological illnesses such as bipolar illness or for treating the biologically depressed person for whom psychotherapy has only slight benefit. The fact that medications have proven effective in the treatment of these disorders does not negate the additional value of psychological treatment. Even when mental illness is treated properly, there are likely to be personal limitations that will diminish a positive response to chemicals. A combination of therapies involving antidepressants, the retraining of social habits, and the adaptation of new lifestyle changes guarantees the most success.[17]

If a patient has not developed many biological symptoms such as weight loss or sleep problems, or the source of the depression is realistically based—dissatisfaction with one's job, unhappy with a marriage, economic problems—psychological therapy might provide the assistance needed to elevate the mood. One of the three mentioned psychological therapies can be very helpful in overcoming various "learned maladaptive behaviors," as can be approaches that emphasize self-monitoring.

One of the drawbacks to psychotherapy is the high cost of treatments. While users of standard antidepressants may pay approximately $80 per month, they may incur charges of twice that amount for a single psychotherapy session. That amount multiplied by four sessions per month, twelve months per year, and the cost for many people can be prohibitive. With many insurance companies limiting the number of sessions covered, patients are often forced to pay their expenses out of pocket or to choose less expensive therapies. The high cost of psychotherapy has also prompted some insurance companies and physicians to recommend drug therapy as a cheaper alternative.

THE HERB FOR DEPRESSION

As you will see in the next chapter, St. John's wort has been shown to be an effective, inexpensive, and safe method of treating certain types of depression. As you read the information keep in mind that this herb is not a panacea. St. John's wort is not meant to be an across-the-board replacement for conventional psychiatric drugs or psychotherapy. St. John's wort is simply another effective medicinal tool for treating depression, albeit one with benefits that other clinical antidepressants do not possess—namely a lack of significant side effects and potential antiviral capabilities.

CHAPTER 4

GETTING RID OF THE BLUES

Karin Taylor's black moods were often accompanied by in-
explicable bouts of insomnia, crying and lethargy. By last
summer she'd sunk so low she didn't care if she lived or died.
But Taylor balked when her physician suggested a common
antidepressant: she didn't feel comfortable taking drugs. For-
tunately, she says, a friend visiting from California sug-
gested a natural herb called Saint John's Wort. Within three
weeks, Taylor's depression had lifted. "I feel restored," says
the 59-year-old Toronto accountant, who continues to take
two herb capsules daily. "I'm my normal self again."

Sue Miller, *Newsweek*

Herbalists in ancient and early modern times used St. John's wort to
ward off apparitions and enchantments as well as to relieve depression
and anxiety. It was widely acknowledged that the tea could soothe
nerves and lift melancholy. But with the rise of modern pharmaceu-
ticals in the nineteenth and twentieth centuries, the herb fell into dis-
use. Recent research, however, has revived interest in this amazing herb,
and a barrage of clinical studies report that, true to the wisdom of the
old herbalists, St. John's wort effectively treats emotional and nervous
complaints.

This is good news for those seeking alternatives to psychiatric drugs
and their potential side effects and for those unable to find relief with
the antidepressants currently on the market. Any person who suffers
from mild to moderate depression is a potential candidate for the

benefits of this herb. Research has concluded that St. John's wort is decidedly more effective than placebos and at least as effective as certain prescription antidepressants in treating milder forms of depression.

This has all come as a surprise to mainstream medical doctors and pharmacologists who have long been skeptical of natural remedies, especially herbal medicines. Research was conducted in response to patients who wanted an alternative to conventional psychiatric drugs. St. John's wort has had a long history of use in Germany, thus people were familiar with it in the way that people in the United States are familiar with the therapeutic applications of garlic. At that time, extracts were sold, but the consumer demand for the products resulted in a push for stronger, more potent extracts, which in turn prompted Licht Wer Pharma to perform clinical studies on the herb. Patients were asking their doctors about the herbal remedy. After several studies showed hypericin to be effective in the treatment of mild depression in clinical trials, doctors felt comfortable in recommending the botanical medicine to patients. German patients who wanted an alternative to conventional psychiatric drugs drove the research in Germany, the country that has spearheaded research on this herb. New clinical studies were conducted in response to the preparation of more potent extracts of Hypericum that already enjoyed widespread sales in the region. Apparently, the patients had a deep mistrust of the synthetic antidepressants and asked their doctors about other, more natural options. Hypericum was their answer.

Thanks in part to Licht Wer Pharma, a small company in Berlin, St. John's wort vaulted into the international spotlight. Everyone now taking St. John's wort owes a debt of gratitude to the German company. In 1992 the company first introduced hypericum pills for the treatment of depression in Germany. The product became an immediate success and captured a 16.4 percent share of the German market for antidepressants. In 1997 that share rose to 27.3 percent.

Experts in both Germany and the United States admit that Licht Wer Pharma played an all-encompassing role in the rebirth of St. John's wort. First, the high dose preparations were a big improvement over the traditional use of teas and oils. Second, "Licht Wer waged an aggressive campaign to establish the herb's scientific credibility by commissioning rigorous studies at independent universities and laboratories."[1] If it were not for this tiny company in Europe, St. John's wort might never have made such an incredible comeback, inspiring numerous clinical studies and helping thousands of people find relief for their depression and anxiety. Nevertheless, pharmacologists and doctors readily acknowledge that there is a notable lack of information available on the herb. No long-term clinical studies have yet been performed on the herb, so there is no information on the herb's effectiveness over a long period of time, and whether the herb can function as a maintenance treatment is still in question. In addition, ideal dosage levels have not been adequately addressed, and the herb's ability to treat severe forms of depression, such as bipolar disorder, is unknown. The matter of side effects also remains unresolved; St. John's wort has at least one known side effect thus far, an increase in photosensitivity.

But these unanswered questions are stimulating a fantastic number of new clinical studies and have not deterred people from purchasing the herb. Indeed, the number of people searching for an alternative remedy to depression has catapulted.

What Is inside the Herb?

Research has identified two primary classes of constituents that make up the herb you and I recognize as St. John's wort, the naphthodianthrones and the flavonoids. The first class contains the chemicals hypericin and pseudohypericin, names with which you are probably familiar. When you pick up a bottle of St. John's wort you will most likely see the phrase standardized for 0.3 percent hypericin content. Though the actual hypericin concentration will vary from manufacturer to manufacturer, some companies prefer to sell standardized extracts of a lesser potency such as 15 percent.

It was once believed that these two ingredients were directly responsible for the herb's medicinal effects. Scientists found evidence that the naphthodianthrones were responsible for the primary antidepressive action of St. John's wort. Hence, hypericin and pseudohypericin became the markers for determining active potency, and clinical studies of St. John's wort used an extract standardized for these chemicals. However, researchers have recently identified many other biologically active substances in the herb, and evidence suggests they all work synergistically. Currently, only hypericin and pseudohypericin are standardized and guaranteed to a certain level (Table 1).

The second class is made up of various flavonoids, a group of biologically active molecules that fall under the umbrella classification of polyphenols. There are twelve categories of flavonoids, of which the best known are the bioflavonoids. The rinds of citrus fruits are a distinctly rich source of bioflavonoids, and manufacturers commonly add bioflavonoids to vitamin C products to potentiate the vitamin's effects, in addition to offering the benefits of flavonoids themselves. The flavonoids present in St. John's wort include proanthocyanidins and quercetin. To give a greater perspective to the function of these two particular flavonoids, grape seed extract and hawthorn berry are two herbs that contain proanthocyanidins, the substances responsible for grape seed's antioxidant actions and hawthorn berry's beneficial effects on cardiovascular disorders. The other flavonoid, quercetin, is naturally present in onions. In clinical studies quercitin has been shown to act as a potent anti-inflammatory.

Although St. John's wort is standardized for the naphthodianthrones, flavonoids play an important role in the herb's antidepressive actions. Continuing research into the exact mechanisms behind the herb's effectiveness is currently trying to determine the extent of the flavonoids' role, and scientists believe they play a much larger one than was originally assumed.

Indeed, scientists hypothosize that all the ingredients in St. John's wort, not just the ones belonging to the two primary classes, work together. No one specific constituent is thought to be responsible for its medicinal effect. According to a statement in the St. John's wort monograph issued by the American Herbal Pharmacopoeia:

> Hypericum contains numerous compounds with documented biological activity. Most researchers consider its effects to be due to a variety of constituents rather than any single component. Constituents that have stimulated the most interest include the naphthodianthrones hypericin and pseudohypericin, a broad range of flavonoids, including quercetin, quercitrin, amentoflavone and hyperin, the phloroglucinols hyperforin and adhyperforin, the essential oil; and xanthones.[2]

As with other plants, hypericum contains many different chemicals, that, alone or in combination with one another, are thought to be responsible for its effects. New research suggests that the chemicals might work better in concert than in isolation, but for the present, the marker constituents, or the compounds by which therapeutic activity is measured, are hypericin and pseudohypericin. Until we know more, the current standardization for hypericin is the best method of ensuring adequate levels of all active constituents.

TABLE 1: THE ROLE OF ACTIVE CONSTITUENTS OF ST. JOHN'S WORT*

CONSTITUENT	ACTIVITY
Amentoflavone	Anti-inflammatory. Found to be effective in the treatment of ulcers.
GABA	Sedative effect.
Hyperforin	Acts as an antibacterial against gram-positive bacteria; wound-healing; inhibits neurotransmitters thus raising their levels; may be effective in the fight against cancer.
Hypericin	Antiviral effect. May also be used to treat cancer.
13, 118-biapigenin	Thought to have a sedative effect.
2-methyl-butenol	Sedative effect.
Proanthocyanidins	Functions as an antioxidant, antimicrobial, antiviral, and blood vessel relaxant.
Quercitin	Antidepressant effect.
Xanthones	Antidepressant effect, antimicrobial, antiviral, diuretic, and helpful in maintaining heart function.

*Upton R. et al. *American Herbal Pharmacopoeia and Therapeutic Compendium.* "St. John's wort: *Hypericum perforatum.*" Santa Cruz, 1997.

FINDING MORE INFORMATION ABOUT ST. JOHN'S WORT

The following are summaries and explanations of some of the most significant clinical studies performed on St. John's wort. I did not list every study available or provide detailed information about certain studies, as compelling as they may be. If you are interested in taking a look at some of the studies in their entirety, refer to the endnotes in the back of the book or contact the American Herbal Pharmacopoeia listed in appendix B to request their monograph on St. John's wort, which includes a substantial listing of available research on the herb. The National Library of Medicine, the medical directory accessible on the World Wide Web, is also a good source for hypericum resources (http://medline.cos.com).

THE FIRST MAJOR STUDY

In August 1996 the *British Medical Journal* published a review of twenty-three controlled studies involving 1,757 patients with mild to moderately severe depressive disorders. The research team included members from both Germany and the United States. This became the mother of all articles, the review that would bring hypericum out of relative obscurity and into the public eye. The publication of "St. John's wort as an antidepressant" is one of the most acknowledged and referred-to articles among the annals of hypericum clinical studies.

The objective of the trials was to investigate whether or not the extract of hypericum was more effective than a placebo in the treatment of depression and to measure its effectiveness against that of standard anti-depressants. A placebo is an inactive substance prepared to look exactly like the active substance being tested. Fifteen of the twenty-three trials were placebo controlled, and were double blind. Double-blind trials are a more reliable scientific method of testing medications and evaluating their efficacy because neither the giver nor the receiver of the substance knows if it is the active medication or the placebo. Only someone not directly involved in dispensing the medication is aware of this information.

One group of patients was administered the extract of St. John's wort while another group of patients, the control group, was fed the inactive substance. At the beginning of each double-blind experiment, the subjects were told that the substance they were receiving might be either the medication or the placebo, ensuring the objectivity of both the researchers and the subjects. The subjects' depressive symptoms were measured at the beginning and at the end of the medication administration period, and a comparison between the two sets of data was then made. A majority of the trials clearly showed that hypericum outperformed the placebo in the treatment of depression, with very few persons experiencing side effects. Of 225 patients in the control group, 94 experienced improvements (22.3 percent). Of 408 patients in the hypericum group, 225 patients responded positively to the herbal medication (55.1 percent). These percentages are significant among general placebo-controlled studies. Indeed, the variation between the two groups provides ample evidence that St. John's wort functions as an antidepressant and is considerably more effective in relieving the symptoms of depression than a placebo.

The other eight trials compared depressive patients taking St. John's wort to those taking standard antidepressants or sedatives. Early trials suggested that the herb was as effective as the standard antidepressants tested, which included maprotiline (Ludiomil), imipramine (Tofranil), desipramine (Norpramin), and amitriptyline (Elavil). (These medications are the classic tricyclic antidepressants that have been used during the last thirty years to treat depression and corresponding anxiety. They increase the levels of serotonin and norepinephrine in the brain by slowing their rate of reabsorption by nerve cells.) Those patients receiving hypericum preparations responded slightly better than those receiving the standard antidepressants. In the hypericum group 63.9 percent of the participants experienced emotional relief versus 58.5 percent of those in the standard antidepressant group. It was further found that, like conventional antidepressants, hypericum extract requires two to four weeks for its mood elevating effects to develop.

Two other trials investigated the efficacy of a combination of hypericum and valerian in comparison to standard antidepressants. Traditional herbalists have long employed valerian *(Valeriana officinalis)* as a sedative to relieve insomnia, stress, and anxiety. Generally regarded as safe and approved for food use by the FDA, valerian is widely available at health food stores throughout the United States. Of the participants taking the herbal remedy, 67.7 percent reported positive responses to the treatment; only 50 percent of those taking standard antidepressants found relief. A whopping difference of 17.7 percent was recorded between the two groups. The results of this study suggest that hypericum may be more effective when combined with valerian for an all-encompassing synergistic effect. Since only two of the twenty-three trials conducted used this particular combination of herbs, however, more evidence is needed before firm conclusions can be drawn. Obviously, more trials of combination remedies are needed.

Side Effects

Total drops-out rates among hypericum users were significantly less than those among antidepressant users. Average rates were determined from the placebo-controlled trials and the trials of the combination of hypericum and valerian. St. John's wort was less likely to produce the unintended and undesirable side effects associated with the conventional tricyclic antidepressants, which include drowsiness, urinary retention, dry mouth, increased heart rate, and sometimes feelings of anxiety or restlessness. No significant side effects were associated with St. John's wort.

In one study, only 2.4 percent of patients taking St. John's wort reported side effects. The side effects described included mild gastrointestinal discomfort, which was relieved by administering the herb with meals and a large glass of liquid; dry mouth; dizziness; fatigue; and skin rashes and itching. The authors suggested that these side effects were rare and mild, although long-term side effects are not known since none of the studies was more than eight weeks in length.

Dutch clinicians Peter de Smet and Willem Nolen agreed the data look promising and commented on the low rate of side effects writing, "The herb may offer an advantage in terms of relative safety and tolerability, which might improve patient compliance. So far, its extensive use in Germany has not resulted in published case reports about serious drug interactions or toxicity after overdose."[4] St. John's wort appears to cause fewer short-term side effects than the conventional drugs, a conclusion supported by additional studies.

Criticisms

The article would be misleading if the researchers only recorded the benefits of St. John's wort and never mentioned any of the studies' limitations. Some of the manufacturers in the health food industry have jumped on the positive media bandwagon, touting the benefits of the herb without acknowledging the relative lack of complete information.

The clinical studies are not perfect and they do contain a number of flaws. First, the studies involved relatively small numbers of patients. Only 1,757 patients participated in the twenty-three trials. More comprehensive studies are needed in order to gain a better and more complete evaluation of St. John's wort's action on depressive illness.

Second, the methodological quality of each study varies. Most of them lacked proper precision because they did not use a single classification system to define and diagnose depressive disorders. In other words, the definition of depression varied from study to study and did not always meet the stringent criteria used in the United States. For example, one researcher's version of severe depression could have been another researcher's version of mild depression. Thus, certain inconsistencies exist among the studies, which may compromise the results. Any so-called improvement may not be an indication of the medication's efficacy since there was no standard classification system by which to measure the improvement. In addition, researchers were concerned primarily with measuring the main effects and side effects. They did not report the more subjective effects of the medications on the patients such as increased self-awareness or improved self-image.

Third, the preparation of hypericum extract differed from study to study. It was administered in a variety of forms from standardized liquid extracts and capsules to tablets made from the raw herb. In addition, the potency of the dose and the amount of the average daily dosage varied from study to study as well. Some patients were given as little as .40 mg of hypericin per day, while others were given as much as 2.7 mg per day (300 to 1000 mg, respectively).

In reviewing these studies, it appears that apples were compared to oranges. The authors acknowledge that further studies need to be conducted in order to compare St. John's wort extracts with conventional antidepressants and to compare different extracts and doses. Though the researchers were pleased with the initial results, they remained cautious about recommending the herb for worldwide use. The efficacy of different preparations and dosages needs to be examined in more detail. In addition, none of the trials that compared hypericum to a synthetic antidepressant lasted longer than six weeks, and the synthetic drugs were delivered in daily amounts below or at the lower end of the usual dose range.

More trials need to be conducted in order to determine how St. John's wort works as a long-term therapy. Studies must determine whether the herb remains effective throughout long-term treatment and how it affects the risk of relapse, common with many conventional drugs. Although few short-term discomforts were reported, the long-term side effects are not known. Fortunately, no long-term adverse effects have been reported in Germany thus far, and the German Commission E has given the extract a clean bill of health.

Conclusions

Conservative in their estimates of the twenty-three trials, the researchers acknowledge that "current evidence is inadequate to establish whether hypericum is as effective as other antidepressants." The authors suggest that "additional trials should be conducted to compare hypericum with other antidepressants in well-defined groups of patients; to investigate long-term side effects; and to evaluate the relative efficacy of different preparations and dosages."[5]

These limitations notwithstanding, evidence from the randomized trials suggests that hypericum extracts are more effective than placebos in the treatment of depressive disorders and that the side-effect profile is favorable when compared to standard drugs. However, no one is able to yet determine whether they are more effective for certain disorders than others. These tests herald the herb's promise. While there are significant inherent weaknesses in the studies, the article has stimulated interest in natural and unconventional healing practices within the medical establishment. Jerry Cott, Ph.D., chief of the Pharmacologic Treatment Research Program at the National Institute of Mental Health, believes that "investigation of purported therapeutic activity of botanicals stands a good chance of leading to new mechanisms and novel treatments."[6]

ST. JOHN'S WORT: SUPERHERB?

Walter E. Mueller, head of the department of pharmacology at the University of Frankfurt, is a leading clinical researcher of St. John's wort. Dr. Mueller and his colleagues at the university conducted a number of experiments showing that the extract of hypericum had a similar effect to that of standard antidepressants, including Prozac. Published in the German journal *Pharmocopsychiatry*, his research indicated that the hypericum extract "appeared to reduce the rate at which brain cells reabsorb an important neurotransmitting chemical called serotonin."[7] That is the mechanism of action behind the SSRIs Prozac, Zoloft, Paxil, and similar drugs.

Dr. Mueller and his colleagues conducted tests carried out in test tubes as well as on rats and revealed another very interesting factor: hypericum extract was effective in reducing the reabsorption of norepinephrine and dopamine, two of the other chemicals thought to influence emotional behavior. The hypericum extract blocked norepinephrine and dopamine, in addition to serotonin, from binding with the extra receptors, thus restoring brain function to normal. In an interview, Dr. Mueller commented, "I don't know of any other antidepressants that inhibit all three systems."[8]

The neurotransmitter norepinephrine is enhanced by inhibiting its reuptake and blocking its breakdown, the action behind TCAs and MAOIs. Irregularities in this neurotransmitter, which regulates alertness and arousal, may contribute to depressed moods and fatigue. Dopamine is a neurotransmitter in the brain thought to be associated with depression and schizophrenia; its levels also affect adrenaline. Dopamine is used extensively by the limbic system, a structure that encircles the brainstem and affects the functioning of emotional aspects of behavior related to survival and one that is affected by antipsychotic drugs. The amazing news about St. John's wort is that it affects all three of the important neurotransmitters.

This is a substantial discovery. If further tests are able to confirm this finding, it will catapult hypericum to superpower status. No substance in the physician's arsenal of medications is similarly capable of multiplicitous modes of action on all three major neurotransmitters: serotonin, norepinephrine, and dopamine. The TCAs influence only two major neurotransmitters, with potentially harsh side effects. The MAOIs are thought to mainly influence serotonin and nonepinephrine but also have potentially adverse side effects in addition to a required, rigid diet. The success of the SSRIs is attributed specifically to their serotonin-enhancing role. While they may be more effective in the treatment of a wider range of depressive disorders than the previous two, St. John's wort has been shown to act in the same capacity. It appears as if hypericum extract is really capable of influencing the entire mental landscape.

A medication that inhibits the reuptake of all three neurotransmitters probably could not have been developed by drug companies because they limit research to synthetic chemicals that interact with the body and mind in predictable ways. In using this desultory method, "truly unique medications are unlikely to emerge," says Dr. Jerry Cott. This is especially true for research in areas where there are no effective drug treatments, such as for cognitive disorders.[9] If new, more effective and powerful substances are to be produced, medicines must be driven by unique mechanisms of action. They must provide more than incremental improvements on existing drugs.

The possible discovery of the mechanism of action behind hypericum portends major changes in the way we understand the brain, drugs, and their effects on the brain. Though the symptoms of depression may be similar from one person to another, the brain chemicals causing the depression may vary—hypericum's ability to inhibit the reuptake of all three neurotransmitters may be its source of superior strength and resultant efficacy.

ST. JOHN'S WORT: MAOI OR SSRI?

In 1984 researchers reported that hypericin operates as a MAOI and attributed the herb's antidepressive effects to this action.[10]

You will recall from chapter 3 that a MAOI inhibits an enzyme called monoamine oxidase, which is found throughout the body. In the brain, the enzyme breaks down the neurotransmitters norepinephrine and serotonin, thought to be influential in affecting mood and behavior. By inhibiting the enzyme that breaks down these two important neurotransmitters, it was supposed that St. John's wort helps to maintain higher levels of these chemicals.

After the amazing news was revealed, a score of newly published herb books and magazine articles in the health food industry touted this new postulation. It looked as if the mechanism of action behind St. John's wort had finally been discovered after hundreds of years, but subsequent tests conducted by other researchers were not able to confirm the MAOI effect.[11, 12] More recent studies have concluded that hypericin only acted as a MAOI when the hypericum extract used was of weak purity with a high concentration of flavonoids. In other, stronger extracts the MAOI effect was not noted.

New research points to the herb's wide range of action. St. John's wort may possess a mild, low-grade MAOI effect, but this inhibition is not sufficient to explain its antidepressant effect. This is important news. Because St. John's wort does not function as a MAOI, one does not need to follow any dietary restrictions. Anyone who takes MAOIs such as Parnate and Nardil must avoid certain foods, alcoholic beverages, and over-the-counter medications, but these rules do not apply to users of St. John's wort.

No MAOI for You!

Hypericum, in part, functions as an SSRI, similar to Prozac and Paxil. Because of this, hypericum should not be taken with a MAOI such as Nardil, Parnate, or Marplan. This information has not been based on clinical studies of hypericum, but on the medical information known about prescription SSRIs and MAOIs. Research has shown that MAOIs and SSRIs do not mix successfully. When administered together, central serotonin syndrome (CSS) can occur, subjecting persons to any number of severe reactions such as dangerous fluctuations in pulse and blood pressure, confusion, rapid pulse, sweating, and disturbed consciousness, which can ultimately result in coma or death. Thus, if you are currently taking any prescription antidepressants, check with your doctor before combining your medication with St. John's wort or before discontinuing it in favor of an herbal remedy. To date there have been no reported cases in which St. John's wort was injuriously mixed with a MAOI.

Anyone who wants to switch between the two medications must allow a necessary lapse time. Unfortunately, no scientist or doctor is sure precisely how long a waiting period is required because virtually no research is available on the subject. Dr. Harold H. Bloomfield and Peter McWilliams, though, make a good suggestion in their book *Hypericum & Depression: Can Depression Be Successfully Treated with a Safe, Inexpensive, Medically Proven Herb Available without a Prescription?* They recommend that "one should wait four weeks before taking any SRIs—prescription or hypericum," when switching from a MAOI. "Until further research is done on how and why hypericum works to alleviate the symptoms of depression, hypericum should be considered an [S]SRI and treated accordingly."[13]

Once scientists have a better idea of the exact mechanisms of action behind St. John's wort, doctors will no longer need to guess the amount of time involved in switching from drug to drug. For now, one would be wise to heed the advice printed on most labels of St. John's wort: hypericum should not be taken by persons currently taking any prescription MAOIs. Until the data are in, particular caution should be taken.

GOOD NEWS FROM SWEDEN

In June 1997 the Swedish journal *Lakartidningen* released information on twenty-five controlled clinical trials in which hypericum extract was compared with a placebo and established antidepressants. The studies confirmed the herb's mood-elevating effect. The scientists reported that 61 percent of depressed patients taking 1.2 mg per day improved on the low dose. And 75 percent of patients taking 2.7 mg per day showed improvements, a high percentage for controlled study. The results are propitious.

As far as side effects were concerned, they were reported to be mild and occurred less frequently than those of standard antidepressants. Scientists acknowledged the herb's low toxicity as one of its beneficial properties—this makes the herb a favorable treatment, especially among those concerned about the side effects of prescription drugs. As in previous studies published in the *British Medical Journal,* scientists were unable to pinpoint how the herb functions in the brain. The effects are thought to be due to a combination of actions, including a low-grade MAOI effect and more pronounced SSRI effects.[14]

THE FEEL-GOOD HERB

During the last fifteen years, many biological psychiatrists have been asking questions about dopamine's role in the temperament of normal people, according to Dr. Peter Kramer. It is thought that dopamine is involved in a wide range of emotional responses including depression. Like serotonin, dopamine exists at different levels in the brain. Since every one of the neurotransmitters work both together and separately, their balance is necessary for homeostasis in the body. If the dopamine levels tip out of balance, various mental disorders have the potential to erupt.

Most of the antipsychotic drugs that affect dopamine levels work by blocking the action of the brain chemical. For example, dopamine-related illnesses such as schizophrenia respond to drugs designed to attach themselves to postsynaptic receptors. These receptors bind to the neurotransmitter dopamine, preventing it from reaching the receptor. Thus the nerve cell activity dependent on dopamine is discontinued.

Scientists are beginning to learn that St. John's wort is capable of promoting an enzyme that breaks down the neurotransmitter dopamine, resulting in higher dopamine levels. In destroying the biogenic amine, higher dopamine levels are created in the brain. Higher dopamine levels affect adrenaline and offer feel-good benefits.

Other studies have also shown St. John's wort to be effective in dopamine blockage. When rats were administered dopamine antagonists, the effect of the herbal medication was blocked.[15] The herb could not alter the behavior of the rats as it had done in previous studies. The scientists concluded that the neurotransmitter dopamine plays an essential role in the herb's antidepressant effect. In the same study, scientists discovered one other piece of evidence integral to St. John's wort's ability to influence dopamine levels. A decrease in serum-prolactin, a hormone that maintains milk secretion, was noticed in the rats as well, providing a further evidence of dopamine manipulation by the herb because the increase of dopamine leads to a decrease in prolactin.[16]

The inhibition of dopamine in addition to the other affected neurotransmitters influenced by St. John's wort shows the herb's unique multiplicitous mode of action in its treatment of depression. Researchers have pointed to the fact that the herbal extract is complex in its action, perceptibly exerting its influence over dopamine levels. The precise influential role of dopamine manipulation by St. John's wort, however, is still somewhat ambiguous and of course, more tests must be conducted. Despite this, the research looks ultimately encouraging.

THE HERB AMAZES SCIENTISTS AGAIN

Fortschr Med, a medical journal published in Germany, featured an article in its September 10, 1995 issue, that confidently recommended the use of St. John's wort as an antidepressant. It must have been quite a surprise to the doctors reading it—the herb had successfully made its way into the scientific journals once again! The summary quote read, "Recent studies have shown that [hypericum] is clinically effective for the treatment of the symptoms of depression. It has proved superior to placebo, equally as effective as standard medication and has a clear advantage over the latter in terms of side effects. It follows that, on the basis of our present knowledge, St. John's wort can be recommended for use as an anti-depressant."[17]

One month later, the same journal published a review of a placebo-controlled, double-blind study in which ninety-seven patients suffering from depression were treated with hypericum extract. In the course of treatment, they were continually evaluated to record their progress and the so-called therapeutic effects of the herb. Seventy percent of the patients responded to the herb (forty-three people), a percentage corresponding to that of standard antidepressants. The journal recorded that the herbal extract was "extremely" well tolerated, and no side effects were reported by any of the patients.[18]

Interestingly, the herbal extract was not only reported to treat depression but it also had an anxiolytic effect on the patients. In other words, St. John's wort was found to reduce anxiety. In discovering this piece of evidence, the scientists unintentionally confirmed the health claims of generations of herbalists who have labeled St. John's wort a nervine herb, capable of soothing the nerves and calming an overactive nervous system. Contemporary science may have proven what traditional herbalists have said all these years.

Various types of anxiety disorders exist—panic disorders, phobias, obsessive-compulsive disorder, post-traumatic stress disorder, and generalized anxiety disorder. It is estimated that half of the people affected by depression also have some type of coexisting anxiety disorder, and different anxiety disorders respond to different forms of treatment. From the research gathered on St. John's wort, the herbal extract is thought to improve the condition of generalized anxiety disorder (GAD). Unlike some of the other anxiety disorders, GAD is not a reaction to an experience, a situational anxiety. Instead, GAD is a condition in which general anxiety expresses itself at any time, on any day, and in any situation. It is much more serious than everyday anxiety, and the disorder is considered pathological. Those who suffer from GAD are always stressed-out, worried, and strung-out. Their concerns may be more illusory than real.

Of course, it is too early to tell if St. John's wort is the definitive herbal treatment for anxiety disorder, but evidence of its potential weighs in its favor. St. John's wort is effective in reducing the secondary symptoms of depression, such as anxiety and insomnia, and enough credible evidence exists for the German Commission E to recommend its use in the treatment of anxiety.

SAFER THAN VALIUM

In the 1970s Valium was the principal drug prescribed to relieve anxiety, and it remained the most popular minor tranquilizer from 1975 to 1980 according to the National Prescription Audit, a group that measures prescriptions dispersed by retail pharmacies across the United States. At the height of its popularity the drug was overprescribed to women who probably had problems that did not warrant the use of the medication. Doctors often recommended Valium as therapeutic treatment for stress or anxiety resulting from boredom, loneliness, or depression. Addictive, its subsequent abuse by patients was widespread.

Valium belongs to the class of drugs called the benzodiazapines, a group of medications commonly prescribed to treat anxiety and insomnia. Some of the more popular benzodiazapenes include Xanax, Klonopin, and Ativan. All of the benzodiazapine drugs used to treat anxiety have been found effective in attaching themselves to the benzodiazapine receptors. In fact, the stronger a benzodiazapine binds to the receptors, the greater its effectiveness in reducing anxiety. Except in their potency and duration of action, there is not a great deal of variety in the effects produced by this class of drugs. A few of the standard medications in this class, however, are useful in the treatment of seizure disorders and depression.

A natural anxiety-reducing substance, St. John's wort has been found to increase the binding power of benzodiazapine receptors, relieving anxiety and producing a mild sedation. Scientists have found that hypericum exhibits a long-term effect on anxiety similar to that of diazepam (Valium) and bromazepam but without the associated dangers of long-term use.[19] While benzodiazapines are very effective drugs, they are extremely addictive and the withdrawal syndrome associated with their discontinuance can be particularly uncomfortable and distressing and sometimes dangerous. Fortunately the potential for addiction to hypericum appears nonexistent. No study has recorded any appearance of withdrawal symptoms after the administration of St. John's wort; so far, no scientist or doctor has seen a physical dependence created by the herbal extract. This is positive news for sure, but until further long-term studies are conducted, no one will be quite sure how long the standardized extract can be safely administered.

Generations of herbalists have persistently recommended the use of

St. John's wort in the treatment of insomnia. Recent clinical studies confirm that hypericum increases deep sleep and decreases the difficulty in falling asleep. The herb is often included in combination with other nervine herbs in many "sleepytime" and "good night" teas and supplements. Barbara and Peter Theiss, authors of *The Family Herbal*, cite St. John's wort as "the most important medicinal herb for insomnia and for the nervous system in general, as well as having many other fields of application."[20] Not surprisingly, patients in the hypericum group in the particular study written about above would definitely agree with the Theiss' statement. The study showed they had a much easier time falling asleep than those taking the placebo.

In a different study conducted and reported in the 1992 issue of the journal *Therapiewoche*, fifty patients underwent a double-blind study with hypericum. The patients treated were diagnosed with neurotic depression and brief depressive reaction in addition to several other unclassified depressive states. Among the standardized measurements used to classify mental states were the Hamilton Depression scale (HAMD) and the Hamilton Anxiety Scale (HAMA). Patients were administered a standardized extract of hypericum or placebo twice per day for a period of eight weeks.

When clinical research trials on medications are conducted, researchers employ a basic classification system, which allows them to diagnose the patient and subsequently chart his or her progression during the treatment. Using an interview technique and observation, physical and emotional symptoms are recorded and turned into numbers. Once the study has ceased, the patient is observed one last time and his or her results are combined according to the standard classification criterion. The HAMD and the HAMA are two standard methodologies that ensure diagnostic precision and objective results. If classification systems were not used, results of studies would be extremely subjective and difficult to rely on.

A rise or drop in the percentage of patients according to the Hamilton score simply means that researchers noted either advancements or declines in the progress of a patient using the classification system as a reference.

At the end of the eight weeks, 80 percent of the participants in the herb group responded to the medication according to the HAMD criteria. Only 44 percent in the placebo group responded according to the same scale. No side effects were noted in either group. A 70 percent drop in the HAMA score was noted after eight weeks in the hypericum group while only a 42.1 percent was seen in the placebo group. The compared percentages show a significant difference between the herb and dummy medication and are consistent with other successful placebo-controlled studies. The double-blind study indicates that St. John's wort is fairly successful not just as an antidepressant medication but also as an anxiolytic.[21]

Of further interest, the improvements in the mood and mental attitude of the patients were much greater after eight weeks of use than after four weeks of use. More than 50 percent of the improvement appeared between weeks four and eight. In fact, scientists speculate that future studies might show the herbal extract to be more effective with long-term use. Patients noted additional improvement during weeks six through eight.

Thus, the effects of hypericum appear to be cumulative, increasing steadily over time, which explains why patients report that the herb becomes "stronger" the longer it is taken. Unlike benzodiazapene drugs that offer relief within an hour of taking the pill, St. John's wort requires a minimum of two to four weeks before effects are noticed. A one-time ingestion of the herb will not produce results. Correspondingly, it is unknown when the effects of hypericum plateau or diminish.

Several theories attempt to explain why the herb must be taken over a period of time in order to yield its uplifting effects. One of them suggests that hypericum needs time to cross the blood-brain barrier. This may also account for St. John's wort's benign side-effect profile, which I will touch on in greater detail later in the chapter.

IT IS CALLED GABA

I had never heard of GABA until I walked into a health food store in the 1980s and asked the clerk what supplement people were taking for anxiety and insomnia. He guided me to where GABA sat on the shelf near fifty other "calm-you-down" supplements. I asked him what it was and how it worked and if he could give me any information on the substance. He responded, "I have no idea exactly what it is, but I sure know that it makes you feel mellow, really laid back. I also know that the name stands for something really long."

GABA is an acronym for gamma-aminobutyric acid, an inhibitory neurotransmitter found in the brain and the spinal chord. Scientists believe that too little GABA could be the cause of anxiety. Basically, GABA's job is to reduce the activity of overfiring nerves it contacts. Antianxiety drugs such as Valium enhance the inhibitory effects of GABA, thus reducing binding to its receptors. When drugs bind to the GABA receptor, the shape of the receptor changes and the cell responds more readily to GABA. Some scientists think GABA assists the receptor-binding activity of the benzodiazapenes, but others suggest that the benzodiazapenes increase the ability of GABA to attach to its own receptor. Regardless of the specific mechanisms, GABA is effective in reducing anxiety and insomnia. Notedly, naturopathic doctors usually recommend GABA as a substitute for standard prescription antianxiety drugs.

The National Institute of Mental Health revealed that St. John's wort exerts a potent affinity for GABA receptors.[22] In 1993 Dr. Jerry Cott reported this at the annual meeting of the American College of Neuropsychopharmacology, and a later study by Mueller et al. confirmed the report. Tests showed that St. John's wort inhibited GABA uptake and GABA receptor binding, although scientists do not have any clear-cut explanation for GABA binding at this time.[23]

GENTLE MICE

In 1987 in Germany, several animal studies conducted on mice with a standardized extract of hypericum revealed interesting results. After mice were treated with the herbal extract, scientists noticed increased physical activity in mice and reduced aggressiveness in isolated male mice.[24] Further, the exploratory activity of mice in foreign environments was increased. The change in activities of the mice after the administration of the extract can be interpreted as an antidepressant effect.

Furthermore, in separate tests conducted in Germany in 1995, in the Porsolt test or the so-called forced swimming test, the extract showed an effect on the mice equal to the effect of the antidepressant imipramine. The Porsolt test is an effective method of measuring the time mice remain immobile in certain stress situations, a way of measuring the "fighting spirit" of mice that lets scientists know exactly how long a mouse will deal with a stressful situation before giving up. This test has been an effective indicator of the antidepressant effect of various pharmaceutical compounds.[25] Similar results to the Porsolt tests were found in tail suspension tests.

In addition, the herbal extract was reported to antagonize the effects of resprine, a drug that depletes the brain of chief neurotransmitters. The authors of the scientific study concluded that hypericum was effective and responsible for the various activities in the animal models; the activities are suggestive of the herb's antidepressant effects.

PUMPED UP HORMONES

St. John's wort has been shown to inhibit certain stress-related responses such as the secretion of cortisol and other hormones. Cortisol, the major hormone produced by the adrenal gland, is concerned with normal metabolism and resistance to stress in the body. Like the other body chemicals, cortisol becomes imbalanced in cases of depression. High levels of this particular hormone can be immune inhibiting. Since they pose a potential threat to the security of the immune system, they must be kept at key accommodation levels.

High cortisol levels are present in depressive states. Recent studies suggest that St. John's wort may act as a cortisol secretion inhibitor, lowering the cortisol levels in the body. It is hypothesized that the herbal extract acts on the hormones including cortisol and the Andreno-corticotropic hormone (ACTH is the stimulating hormone that causes the adrenal cortex to secrete cortisol) by inhibiting immune modulators referred to as cytokines.[26] As you will see shortly, the drop in cortisol levels is related to a corresponding inhibition of cytokines.

WORKING THROUGH THE IMMUNE SYSTEM

A cytokine is a soluble factor released or secreted by the cells, which affects the activity of other cells. Whereas neurotransmitters relate to one another through the transmission of ions, as we learned earlier, cytokines relate in a more physical manner. There are several varieties of cytokines, including the interleukins, which are among the most recognized. The cytokines play a significant role in the proper functioning of the immune system through the promotion of cell growth and cell reproduction.

Researchers have long been aware of the role neurotransmitters such as norepinephrine and serotonin play in depression and other mental illnesses, but other important physiological factors may equally influence the makeup of the disease. One of these other factors could be the immune system. Interestingly, there are only two biological structures in the body that possess some sort of memory capacity: the central nervous system and the immune system. Scientists are aware that there are many interactions between these two structures. Responsible for a portion of this activity is the secretion of various hormones and certain cytokines. Researchers have pointed out that, "cytokines are heavily involved in the communication between cells inside and outside the immune system, especially in the nervous system."[27] The brain or the endocrine organs influence almost every manifestation of the immune system either directly or indirectly.

Anytime the immune system is activated, it must be assumed that a causal change in neural or endocrine function is responsible. The changes the scientists refer to include loss of appetite, fever, and drowsiness.

Scientists guess that various types of cytokines, or more specifically, certain interleukins, are capable of creating the symptoms recognized as depression. Different cells, which are stimulated by different sorts of stimuli such as infections or allergies or estrogen, lead to increased levels of interleukins and result in changes in the mental state. What you and I recognize as depressive illness then shows up in the individual.

Results of the studies reinforced the theories put forth by the authors. Based on the research, they came to the conclusion that cytokines affect the nervous system in both direct and indirect ways. One particular interleukin (IL-1) had an effect on slow-wave sleep and appetite loss. The influence of hypericum on this specific interleukin might also influence a more effective serotonin reuptake inhibition.[28] Two other interleukins (IL-1B and IL-6) induced the production of the hormones ACTH, CRH, and cortisol. The production of one of the hormones, CRH, dangerously stimulated the production of IL-6, the same interleukin responsible for the hormone's creation. As a result, a vicious circle was created in the body, each substance stimulating the production of the other and prolonging the depressive illness.

After the research was completed, scientists felt confident in remarking that St. John's wort appeared to reduce the IL-6 excretion responsible for the production of the hormones, which in turn reduced their secretion and levels in the body.[29] The original hypothesis appears valid:

the herbal extract works in conjunction with the neurotransmitters and the immune system.

SEASONAL AFFECTIVE DISORDER

During the winter months, many people find their emotions taking a nosedive, but others become seriously depressed, affected by a condition known as Seasonal Affective Disorder (SAD). From the time of Hippocrates, the winter blues has appeared in the annals of medical history. SAD is an annual cycle of depression that regularly occurs in the autumn and winter months and disappears in the spring and summer. It appears that the disease is linked to seasonal variations in light; the people affected are abnormally sensitive to these changes. While the shorter, often gloomy days may affect everyone's emotions to some extent, a few people become significantly more depressed at this time.

Those affected by SAD experience changes in mood, energy, weight, appetite, and sleep patterns. Again, while these may occur in everyone to varying degrees, in patients with SAD these symptoms reach a heightened state of intensity.[30] Unlike classic depressives, SAD patients commonly experience somnolence, weight gain, and changes in eating habits, marked by an increased preference for carbohydrate-containing foods. Approximately 3 percent to 5 percent of the population suffers from SAD. Light therapy, treatment with bright, full spectrum light, is the main treatment for this type of depression. According to initial studies on St. John's wort and SAD, the herbal extract may be of assistance.

Exactly how seasonal and daily cycles of light and dark affect the brain is unknown. It is thought that melatonin, the brain hormone secreted by the pituitary gland, may play a key role. You have probably heard of this sleep-inducing hormone that was the rave of the health food industry in 1997. Melatonin supplements are primarily taken for their effect on insomnia. While melatonin is considered to have many applications, its prime importance is the regulation of biological rhythms such as sleep and sexual activity. Some scientists believe that disturbances in biological rhythm are due to insufficient melatonin secretion; others believe SAD has more to do with disruptions in serotonin or thyroid hormone.

The first study of its kind, a four-week trial was conducted on twenty patients who were diagnosed with Seasonal Affective Disorder. Each received a combination of light therapy and hypericum extract. Researchers recorded a significant decrease in total symptomatology for the whole group. Feelings of despondency, fatigue, desire for action, and bad temper were noted to improve over time. None of the patients experienced any adverse drug reactions.[31]

The results of the test look positive, but the researchers are aware that the study included a very small number of patients. Placebo-controlled trials on larger subject groups are necessary before St. John's wort can be touted as the definitive treatment for SAD. At this time, it appears that the herb may be a suitable adjunct to the application of light therapy; more specifically, the mood-elevating effects of hypericum might be increased by the use of bright lights. The scientists also mention that St. John's wort might be an alternative to light therapy.

Another study combining light therapy and hypericum extract confirmed the possibility that hypericum possesses a light-sensitizing mechanism. It was found that "the nocturnal secretion of melatonin increased significantly after medication [hypericum extract]."[32] Interestingly, the MAOI family of antidepressants is also known to increase levels of nocturnal melatonin. So do desipramine (Norpramin and Pertofrane) and fluvoxamine (Luvox) and Lithium.[33]

In Dr. Russel J. Reiter's book, *Your Body's Natural Wonder Drug: Melatonin,* he cites several studies that corroborate melatonin's action as a mood elevator. For instance, the amino acid tryptophan, from which melatonin is derived, has been shown to increase melatonin levels. An increase in melatonin production along with a substantial antidepressive effect was noted in studies involving the amino acid.

Melatonin and serotonin are close cousins, and Dr. Reiter explains, "In some respects, melatonin is a more logical candidate as a treatment for depression. Serotonin has difficulty crossing the blood-brain barrier. Therefore, to increase the activity of serotonin in the brain, pharamacologists have to concoct drugs that block the enzymatic destruction of the compound or prevent it from being reabsorbed by neurons. But to increase melatonin levels in your brain, all you have to do is take melatonin."[34]

The reasons SAD people experience weight gains and crave carbohydrates are still being explored.[35] One theory is that eating carbohydrates raises the levels of tryptophan in the brain, a step in the synthesis of serotonin. Another theory points to melatonin levels. As Dr. Reiter pointed out, an increase in the amino acid tryptophan stimulated melatonin production in studies.

Given this evidence and the studies performed with St. John's wort on SAD, it is reasonable to assume that the herb is a powerfully complex cocktail capable of affecting depressive illness on many levels. Though more studies should be performed on SAD patients, the evidence in favor of hypericum extract looks promising.

THE LANDMARK STUDY ON 3,250 PATIENTS

The largest study ever conducted on St. John's wort and its use in the treatment of depressive illness was comprised of 3,250 patients. Hailed as one of the landmark studies performed to date on the herbal extract, the results are extensive. Magazine and newspaper articles on the herb often cite this study because it offers a more complete and satisfactory description of the improvements experienced by the participants, details that some of the smaller, more simplistic trials lack. Entitled "Benefits and Risks of the Hypericum extract LI 160: Drug Monitoring Study with 3,250 Patients," this study appeared in the *Journal of Geriatric Psychiatry and Neurology* in October 1994.

In a German study, 663 private practitioners and 3,250 patients participated in a four-week treatment session. Of the patients, 49 percent were diagnosed with mild depression; 46 percent with intermediate, or moderate depression; and 3 percent with severe depression (only fifty-six patients were diagnosed with this more serious form of depression). Approximately three times as many women were treated as men. The mean age of the participants was fifty years, with none less than twenty years or more than ninety years of age. Among the most common complaints besides mood and depression were restlessness, difficulty falling asleep, difficulty in staying asleep, headaches, cardiac symptoms, sweating, and gastrointestinal symptoms.

At the end of treatment, the proportion of improvement was impressive. About 80 percent of patients experienced significant improvements or were symptom free. When measured by a different classification system, the percentage was between 60 and 70 percent. These results are comparable to the other studies on hypericum in the journal and about the same as those studies that compared the effectiveness of hypericum to that of tricyclics and other synthetic antidepressants. At the end of the study, improvements were noted in gastrointestinal symptoms, sweating, cardiac symptoms, headaches, sleeping difficulties, restlessness, and depression.[36] However, measured by the first scale, only a small percentage of patients were completely free of symptoms after the four weeks, and about 15 percent of patients were unchanged or worse at the end of the study.

The ages of the participants was divided into four separate groups. At the end of the study, scientists concluded that the effectiveness of the herbal extract did not correlate with the age of the patient. St. John's wort worked equally well in all four age groups (up to 35, 35–50, 51–65, over 65). The scientists wrote, "Efficacy does not depend on age to any obvious extent."[37] Thus, it appears that a thirty-year-old will obtain the same results from the herbal medication as might an eighty-year-old. Further, gender did not seem to influence efficacy. Though more women participated in the study than men, both responded equally positively to the medication.

Side Effects

As in other studies on hypericum, an exceedingly low number of patients experienced side effects Only 2.4 percent (seventy-nine patients) of the 3,250 patients reported side effects, all of which were rare and mild. Side effects included gastrointestinal symptoms (.55 percent), allergic reactions (.52 percent), fatigue (.40 percent), anxiety (.26 percent), dizziness (.15 percent), and other (.55 percent).

The gastrointestinal symptoms reported as side effects of hypericum administration are "somewhat questionable in view of their frequency in depression."[38] Since they occur often in depressive illnesses, they are probably not indicative of a side effect of the herb: 50 percent of patients already exhibited gastrointestinal symptoms before taking St. John's wort. The allergic reactions, one of the other side effects, on the other hand, are related to the medication. No participants in this study experienced a photosensitizing effect. This effect, however, has been found in cattle that graze heavily on the herb. (I will touch on this subject later in the next chapter.)

To better understand the side effects of hypericum, "the frequency of side effects with the hypericum preparation must be compared with the rate of undesired drug effects with synthetic antidepressants."[39] Again, only 2.4 percent of patients experienced adverse reactions in the hypericum study. In drug studies, particularly a recent study in which one of the newer synthetic antidepressants was administered, an average of 19 percent experience undesired effects, which vary in intensity. When the side effects of the herbal extract are compared to the frequency and seriousness of side effects of prescription drug antidepressants, the side-effect rate of hypericum is only about one-tenth, significantly lower. In addition, the dropout frequency in the 3,250 patient study was 1.45 percent compared to an average dropout frequency of 3 to 12 percent, depending on the type of symptom, with standard drugs.

Comments on the Study

The high percentage of improvement coupled with the extremely low rate of side effects make hypericum extract a favorable treatment for depression. Both mild and moderate depressives responded equally to the herb. Had the study continued, perhaps the percentage of patients who improved would have been greater due to the herb's cumulative effects. This, of course, is merely conjecture but a valid one when based on the evidence of several studies, one of which was recorded earlier, and on the comments of doctors on the herb's performance. The 3,250-person study remains one of the most important studies in the continuing investigation of hypericum. Hopefully more studies of this magnitude will be conducted in the future.

SEVERE DEPRESSION

Most of the studies conducted on St. John's wort extract validated its efficacy in the treatment of mild and moderate depressive disorders and anxiety. Consequently, doctors primarily recommend hypericum for the treatment of mild to moderate depressions. However, these studies generally neglected to investigate the herbal extract's potential to treat serious depression. For instance, in the previously mentioned 3,250-person trial, only 3 percent of those patients were diagnosed with severe depressive disorders, a percentage too small to suggest any legitimate conclusions about the herb's efficacy in treating this type of mental disorder. Other studies also excluded most patients suffering from severe depression. Thus the medical establishment and the scientific community are not yet in a position to make any specific claims on the herb's value in this area.

A 1997 study by Ernst-Ulrich Vorbach and colleagues in Germany suggests that St. John's wort is effective in the treatment of serious depressions. The scientists found the herbal extract to be superior in the treatment of serious depression to the commonly used tricyclic drug imipramine. In view of patient tolerance and side effects, hypericum clearly came out ahead.[40]

The authors concluded that more studies need to be run to discover the optimum dose of the herbal extract because the dose-response relationship has not yet been established. Dosage levels of hypericum in most other trials were quite low but in Vorbach's study, it was quite high, the daily dose being 300 mg, three times a day standardized at 3 percent, equivalent to 2.7 mg per day for six weeks. Moderate doses of the imipramine were used in the study to maintain the double-blind structure; otherwise the pronounced side effects of the drug would have revealed to researchers or patients which medications were being administered.[41]

Since the higher dose of hypericum was found effective, the herb's restriction to mild or moderate depressions needs to be reconsidered. New tests must examine the effects hypericum on severe depression, considering extract potency, dose, and duration of treatment. In addition, comparative studies using higher doses of imipramine are necessary.

THE BLOOD-BRAIN BARRIER

In a test conducted on rabbits and mice with the hypericum extract, scientists attempted to discover exactly how hypericum is taken up into the tissues and biodistributed throughout the brain and body. The animals were first injected with the extract, and later the amounts of hypericum in blood and body tissues were measured and examined at various intervals in time. After the experiment, the scientists came up with some very interesting theories that may shed light on the reasons St. John's wort offers a minimum of side effects when administered to persons in therapeutic amounts and on the length of time it takes to achieve a therapeutic effect.

But first, in order to understand the concept of biodistribution of medication more clearly, allow me to explain the chain of events neurological drugs must undergo in the process of biodistribution. The first event is the absorption of the drug. This refers to the mechanism by which drugs pass from the point of entry into the bloodstream. A route of administration is chosen for the drug (oral, rectal, topical), in addition to a proper dose and dosage form (liquid, capsule, tablet) that will allow the drug to be pharmacologically effective and maintain its concentration for a necessary period of time.

Once the drug has been absorbed, it is distributed throughout the body via circulating blood. Within one minute circulation time, it is distributed throughout the circulatory system. Interestingly, most of the administered drug does not reach its preferred site of action and is found elsewhere in the body. This wide distribution throughout the body is the reason for many side effects of drugs.

In most of the body, the capillary membranes have pores that allow drug molecules to pass out of blood capillaries into tissues and vice versa. The brain, however, has a unique structured barrier that does not allow simply any drug to pass. This sheath of protection is called the blood-brain barrier (BBB), and psychoactive drugs are able to penetrate the BBB. By definition they are lipid soluble since they exert their action after passing the BBB.[42]

It is unclear whether or not hypericum passes through the BBB. Yet, in the study headed by Dr. Chung, scientists demonstrated that hypericin passes over to the brain in very small concentrations.[43] The elimination of hypericum in brain tissue (along with the skin and stomach, other organs that are supposed to benefit from hypericum) seems to be extremely slow. The reason for this may have something to do with the herb's molecular weight. Every chemical in nature has a molecular weight. When the molecular weight of a medication is high, its release to the rest of the body is slow. The reason hypericum has such a "slow, steadily increasing effect on depression" may ultimately be due to its molecular weight and correlative distribution half-life. Half-life is a pharmacologic term used to describe the time it takes for a medication to decrease by half its original amount. The diagrams on hypericum suggest its half-life is several weeks.

For the first few weeks, little of the herbal extract reaches its destination. Since it takes several weeks for half of the medication to break down, a constant supply is slowly released to the brain. Scientists believe that hypericum is capable of achieving its antidepressive and anxiolytic effect after many weeks of administration precisely because its half-life is so remarkably long. To give an example of a half-life span for conventional drugs, the half-life of various benzodiazapenes ranges from six hours to two days in length and that of Prozac ranges from seven to fifteen days.

In order to receive the benefits of the St. John's wort extract, the patient must continue taking the medication regularly because the concentrations are released extremely slowly. Typically, a minimum of four weeks treatment with hypericum is suggested. It is likely that the brain concentration of hypericum continues to rise for a long time until it reaches a beneficial level. For any medication to achieve a therapeutic level, enough of it must be delivered into the bloodstream to be effective. If one stops taking St. John's wort, the supply of chemicals delivered to the brain will be depleted and the effects will disappear.

In general, side effects have the potential to be more severe when a substantial amount of medication is present in the body. St. John's wort's extremely long half-life might explain its low side-effect profile. Drugs with a short half-life are more likely to precipitate withdrawal symptoms. The slow rate of accumulation of hypericum in the brain "leaves other areas in the body less exposed to possible effects on the serotonin metabolism in other parts of the body," according to one study conducted by Mueller et al. Thus, the herbal medication accumulates in the necessary tissues over a period of time, while it passes through the other parts of the body quickly. The propensity for side effects is greatly decreased. Incidentally, forgetting to take St. John's wort for a day or two will not cause any side effects, in contrast to certain prescription drugs.

FUTURE STUDIES

Hypericum is now being made the subject of clinical trials here in the United States. The worldwide focus on the herb with yellow flowers has turned a few leading heads among Washington bureaucrats; hypericum appears to have garnered partial acceptance by conventional medicine.

The Office of Alternative Medicine a branch of the National Institutes of Health (NIH), National Institute of Mental Health, and the Office of Dietary Supplements, are joining forces to fund the first U.S. study on *Hypericum perforatum*. The goal is to determine the potential benefits and risks of using the herbal extract in the treatment of depression.[44] Participants in the three-arm, double-blind study (336 people; 112 in each group) will have been diagnosed with mild to moderate depression; they will be administered a standardized extract of hypericum, placebo, or the antidepressant prescription drug Sertraline (an SSRI). The test will last thirty-six months, a far longer time period than some of the two- to six-week tests on hypericum that have been conducted so far. The study will be divided up into two phases: the first phase, or "acute efficacy," which will evaluate the effects of the herbal extract in the short term, that is., eight weeks; and the second phase, which will examine the herb's long-term effects. At the time of this book's release, the test will already be underway.

The thirty-six-month study should raise some interesting questions and offer new information. The length of the study will permit the doctors to explore several essential issues in hypericum treatment such as dose-effect relationship and potential long-term side effects. Since the herb's mood-elevating effects seem to intensify over time, I am curious to see how the herb fares after thirty-six months. Questions that will be raised in the study may include:

What potency is optimal in the treatment of long-term, low-grade depression?

What potency is optimal in the treatment of mild to moderate major depression?

How long a period of time does the herb continue to "get stronger"? Through the tenth week? The twelfth week?

Should initial treatment begin with high doses of the herbal extract in order to achieve steady-state levels in the bloodstream and organs more rapidly?

At what point do the patients become develop a tolerance to the herbal remedy?

Are there side effects after long-term use?

When can an individual stop taking hypericum without relapsing into depression or anxiety?

Does the medication simply relieve mental depression, or does it cure the disorder?

Answers to these questions will contribute to the basic understanding of St. John's wort's influence over neurological states.

WHERE WILL ST. JOHN'S WORT STUDIES LEAD?

Nearly every author of every study conducted on hypericum confirms the need for future studies. If hypericum is to be touted as a modern medication effective in the treatment of depression and anxiety disorders, then scientific research must validate initial claims. Scientists agree that uniformity among the hypericum tests must be accomplished. The dose-effect relationship needs to be explored and established. Until now, it has been tentatively established at best. Further clinical testing is needed to make valid comparisons between standard antidepressants and the herbal extract.

As additional studies provide new information about St. John's wort, scientists will attain a better understanding of the herb's advantages and drawbacks, and doctors will more effectually direct its course of treatment. The contemporary and growing body of research on *Hypericum perforatum* cannot be ignored. These tests comprise only the beginning of research on the plant with yellow flowers. Every major discovery so far has acted as a catalyst for other institutions to pursue their own projects and studies, and we can expect to see many more studies in the future.

CHAPTER 5

A Renewed Sense of Pleasure and Joy

In this refulgent summer it has been a luxury to draw the breath of life. The grass grows, the buds burst, the meadow is spotted with fire and gold in the tint of flowers. The air is full of birds, and sweet with the breath of the pine, the balm-of-Gilead, and the new hay. Night brings no gloom to the heart with its welcome shade. Through the transparent darkness the stars pour their almost spiritual rays. Man under them seems a young child, and his huge globe a toy.

Ralph Waldo Emerson

Anyone taking a drug or herb should endeavor to learn as much as possible about it. What are the effects of the medication? Does it have potential side effects? Should it be taken under the supervision of a doctor or herbalist? Not only should a medication be subject to the evaluations of clinical studies, but it should also undergo a rigorous examination by the potential patient as well. It is in the patient's best interest to assume an active role in the healing process and to educate him- or herself about the disease and potential treatments, including behavioral changes.

This chapter explains the administration of St. John's wort in detail, including combining hypericum with other drugs and herbs, recommended dosage levels, and potential side effects. Becoming aware of these important aspects of treatment will arm St. John's wort users with the knowledge necessary to assume a proactive role in their health and well-being.

WHO CAN TAKE ST. JOHN'S WORT?

Most studies of the effects of St. John's wort extract on depression, indicate that the herb is considerably more effective in relieving mild to moderate depression than a placebo. Several of these studies suggest that some individuals respond better to the herbal extract than to certain standard prescription antidepressants. Even though clinical studies indicate that hypericum is effective in treating mild to moderate depressive states and anxiety, it has not yet demonstrated a clear effect on severe depression.

Any individual suffering from mild to moderate depression may become a user of St. John's wort. In order to recognize if you or someone you know fits the symptoms, an initial consultation with a mental health practitioner is in order. For example, earlier in the book I mentioned that many people are affected by chronic low-grade depression and are not aware that their low feelings constitute a mental disorder. A visit to a doctor or therapist can shed light on the condition.

According to the official German Commission E monograph on St. John's wort, psychovegetative disturbances, depressive states, fear, and nervous disturbances are clinical indications for use of the extract. While the herb is recommended in the treatment of mild to moderate depression in this report, it is also suggested for other disorders, including anxiety. Clinical studies have suggested the ability of hypericum to relieve anxiety and to relieve secondary symptoms of depression, such as headache, sweating, heart palpitations, exhaustion, and insomnia.

Keep in mind, however, that this report was published by the German government. Because herbs are sold and regulated as a dietary supplements in the United States, the FDA is not in a position to approve or disapprove of their use. Under the pretense of being sold as food, dietary supplements do not require specific documentation of their safety or efficacy. This information is only required for prescription drugs. Because St. John's wort is classified as a dietary supplement, only limited structure/function claims can be made on its label, and only if the claims have reasonable scientific validation. Labels of many supplements on the market carry a disclaimer noting that the product has not been evaluated and approved by the FDA.

In Germany, doctors recommend the herb three to one over Prozac. St. John's wort is the first medication commonly suggested for mild to moderate depression and anxiety. In the event a patient does not respond positively to the herbal extract, doctors turn to the standard drugs for use in treatment. Although St. John's wort has not been confirmed in the treatment of severe depression, doctors in Germany have prescribed the herb for this type of depression. Because of its low incidence of side effects and its apparent cumulative effects, it appears worthy as a first try. When used in the clinical treatment of severe depression, however, the herbal extract is prescribed at significantly higher doses than those used in the clinical studies.

CAVEAT EMPTOR

Initially, Germans excited about St. John's wort alleged ability to relieve depression, pressured their doctors for prescriptions. Apparently, the appeal is contagious and has spread across the Atlantic Ocean to the United States where everyone is curious about this herb. After the news program *20/20* aired a feature presentation on St. John's wort extract in June 1997, information specialists at the Herb Research Foundation received more than 4,500 calls. Among the many questions asked, people chiefly wanted to know how they could get the herb.

The media focus on St. John's wort is startlingly similar to the fame that befell the prescription drug Prozac. After Prozac hit a high level of popularity, patients waltzed in to their doctors' offices demanding prescriptions for it. If they did not receive a prescription, they might leave and find another doctor willing to prescribe the drug. Some potential patients read so many articles that hyped the prescription drug and saw so many news features on the television that they felt they were perfect candidates for the drug.

Not immune to the hype, doctors sometimes prescribed the drug too quickly on the basis of insufficient information. If a person felt uneasy and a bit unsatisfied in life, a prescription for Prozac was written. It was easy, effective, and quick.

Likewise the media has made St. John's wort the focus of attention at health food stores, dinner tables, and doctor consultations across the country. People, hearing that hypericum treats the blues and offers a quick lift, are clamoring for the herb.

However, clinical depression is radically different from the normal ups and downs of life. Everybody experiences the blues and periods of anxiety once in a while, but St. John's wort is not a magic bullet that will take away the mental pains of the day when taken once or twice.

Unfortunately, many companies in the health food industry have oversold the herb to the lay public in an effort to reap rewards of the latest fad. Thus, it is the responsibility of consumers to inform themselves about the supplements they take.

To Be or Not to Be under a Doctor's Care?

Since St. John's wort is regulated as a dietary supplement, it is available without a prescription. Anyone can walk into a health food store, supermarket, or pharmacy, and purchase the herb. Seeing a wide variety of herbs on shelves everywhere has undoubtedly left some consumers convinced that they pose no potential dangers to health.

Many herbs have been used safely for centuries by lay people—a cup of peppermint tea to settle an upset stomach, for example, or arnica ointment applied to a bruise. However, the opinion that all herbs, vitamins, and other over-the-counter products are harmless, consistently safe products is simply not sensible. Natural does not always equal safe. The herb ma huang, for example, has been implicated in the cause of several deaths in the United States. High doses of senna leaf have also been viewed as a contributory factor in the deaths of several persons taking a certain weight-loss product. Belladonna is also a natural herb but a very poisonous one. Those who use herbs should take the time to educate themselves about an herb's potential benefits and dangers; no one should ingest a substance—natural or synthetic—without being informed.

The wide availability of St. John's wort leaves plenty of room for people to make their own decisions about self-medication. St. John's wort appears to be a safe and effective herb; serious side effects seem rare, and no deaths have been attributed to its use. Indeed, herbalists have long used it in teas, tinctures, and oils without ill effects. However, new commercial preparations are much more concentrated than raw forms of the herb, and research has determined that hypericum has the potential to alter the neurotransmitter levels in the brain. Thus, attempting to self-diagnose and treat depression, a serious mental disorder, with the long-term use of a standardized form of St. John's wort is quite different from having a calming cup of herbal tea.

The administration of hypericum is still in the experimental stages. Most doctors have not had the opportunity to work with the herb for long enough to predict its effects and determine its reliability in various depressive disorders. In one of the clinical studies conducted on the herbal extract, patients experienced increased effects of the extract into the eighth week of treatment. This was a surprise to the authors of the study. Had the study been extended, would patients have reported an improvement in mood that continued past the eighth week? No one is sure. For these very reasons, medical supervision during the administration of the herb is essential.

If you suffer from mild to moderate depression and plan to take St. John's wort for at least four weeks, you should see a physician. Case management of chronic conditions can be complicated, and the training of a professional is required to steer the patient toward a state of improved health. This is especially true in the management of a serious illness such as depression. A physician will regularly monitor the progress of the patient during the term of treatment, including an evaluation of vital signs such as blood pressure, heart rate, and temperature, sleep patterns, mood and energy levels, and general blood chemistries. The informed physician is also in a better position to establish a safe and effective dosage for the patient. The dosage may need to be scaled back or increased depending on the specific reactions of an individual patient. Third, a physician will be more prepared than a patient for any complications that may arise during treatment. If the patient becomes more depressed after treatment with St. John's wort, the physician will employ his or her professional judgment to assess how the patient is progressing. Other antidepressant drugs may need to be combined with the herbal extract, a therapy that only a doctor should prescribe. An understanding of drug "cocktailing" is beyond the layperson's realm of experience.

Even with medication, some types of depression fail to improve. Psychotherapy can be a helpful adjunct to treatment with St. John's wort. At the very least, frequent follow-up contact with a physician is important. A physician with years of clinical experience can do far more to assist a patient than the latter's attempt to both self-diagnose and self-medicate.

If you plan to take the herb for a short period of time (less than four weeks), a physician's supervision is not absolutely necessary. Yet it is in your best interest to consult with a physician at least once to determine if you are clinically depressed and to ask about dosage levels and corresponding length of treatment.

WORKING WITH A
NATUROPATHIC DOCTOR OR HERBALIST

Many conventional doctors are unfamiliar with the practice of botanical medicine, so it might prove difficult for them to advise patients who wish to be treated with herbs. Some doctors may outright oppose the use of botanical medicine, denouncing its practice as quackery and refusing to assist any patient interested in the alternative therapy. Patients of such doctors might want to seek supervision from practitioners specifically trained in the field of holistic and botanical medicine, namely naturopathic medical doctors or qualified herbalists.

Naturopathic physicians are, for the most part, licensed primary care/ general practice family physicians. Providing complete diagnostic and therapeutic services similar to modern conventional physicians, naturopaths are capable of treating persons in much the same way as conventional doctors with one fundamental difference: their scope of treatments. Trained in clinical nutrition, botanical medicine, homeopathy, psychotherapy, in addition to other "natural" healing techniques, they are not limited to orthodox practices. Naturopaths look for emotional, physical, dietary, environmental, and genetic factors in a person's life that could explain illness, and they suggest practical lifestyle changes that will help prevent chronic disease. Naturopaths will be familiar with herbs like St. John's wort, as well as their use in treatment.

The failure of modern medicine to treat certain diseases, and the increased public awareness of health maintenance, has stimulated the growth of naturopathic medicine. However, at this time naturopathic physicians are licensed in only eleven states (Alaska, Arizona, Connecticut, Hawaii, Maine, Montana, Oregon, Utah, Vermont, and Washington). Those who practice in unlicensed states are limited to the procedures they can legally perform. If you are interested in locating a naturopathic physician, consult the reference section in the back of the book. Several organizations have been listed, along with their addresses, phone numbers, and brief descriptions of their services.

Another alternative to the conventional Western doctor is the herbalist. Unlike naturopathic doctors, herbalists specialize solely in the field of botanical medicine, although some are familiar with the other specialties of naturopathy. Because no governing body licenses herbalists in the United States, their qualifications to treat with herbs vary. In the United Kingdom, herbalists undergo formal training in botanical medicine and licensing, becoming specialists in the area of herbal medicine. Despite their license to practice botanical medicine in the United Kingdom, they are not allowed the same privileges here.

Not everyone in the United States can go to England and receive licensing, so a number of qualified herbalists practice with no formal "credentials," but most are just as competent and knowledgeable as their colleagues overseas. Many occupy positions in the health food industry, formulating herbal combinations for herb companies, owning and operating health food stores, writing professionally on herbs and natural subjects, lecturing at trade shows, running home-study schools, and manufacturing supplements for the industry. Though their expertise may go largely unrecognized by proponents of conventional medicine, these herbalists are well respected by those in the alternative medicine field, including naturopathic doctors. To find an herbalist in your area, consult the reference section at the back of the book. Or visit your local health food store. Some stores offer classes in herbs that lead up to a certification. Some retain an herbalist as a member of the staff.

Length of Treatment

Clinical studies have not recommended a specific time frame for treatment with St. John's wort. Since no long-term research on hypericum has been conduced thus far, no doctors or scientists have been able to provide a definitive answer. Therefore, the length of treatment will vary from person to person.

The average period of depression lasts a few months. The effects of St. John's wort may be noticed in as little time as two weeks. From that point on, its beneficial effects apparently continue. As with any medication, the patient taking hypericum must be sensitive to the mental, emotional, and physiological changes noticed. In addition, a physician should monitor those using the herb for four weeks or more in order to observe their clinical state. The patients' increased self-awareness and repeated visits to the doctor for additional monitoring will assist in establishing a suitable time frame for treatment.

Some patients may experience significant relief in a short period of time. If a person appears to be improving after four weeks, a physician may decide that the patient should continue taking the medication for an additional month's time and then taper off the herbal extract gradually. Others may need to take St. John's wort for considerably longer than two or three months. Some people fail to notice any improvements until six weeks after administration. In this scenario, it may be in a patient's best interest to take the medication for a longer time period than two months.

Unfortunately, these vague guidelines will need to suffice for the time being. When the results of the National Institutes of Health's thirty-six-month study are released, we will learn more about optimal lengths of treatment. Currently, most doctors and scientists recommend that the administration of St. John's wort not exceed eight to twelve months. Until we are more certain of its long-term physiological and neurological effects, treatment should not last longer. If the depression returns, hypericum treatment can be safely restarted after taking a break.

THE MANY FACES OF HYPERICUM

Yesterday afternoon I visited a local pharmacy and browsed through their hypericum section. I found many different bottles of St. John's wort manufactured by various companies. To my surprise, almost every product on the shelf contained a different dosage of the herb. Some bottles listed "300 mg tablet—0.15% standardized hypericin"; another read, "500 mg capsule—Pure St. John's wort"; yet another read, "300 mg tablet—0.3% standardized hypericin." Other supplements contained a combination of five to ten herbs along with St. John's wort. In addition, St. John's wort is offered in many different forms: capsules, tablets, tinctures, teas, extracts, raw herb, and oils. For a consumer, buying St. John's wort can be a confusing process. Which preparation of St. John's wort is most effective in the treatment of depression?

The Standardized Version

The best form of St. John's wort to use in the treatment of depression or anxiety is the standardized, not the raw, version. Earlier in chapter 2,

I explained that the standardization of an herb implies that one or more of the marker compounds in the herb will be present in exact levels. St. John's wort, is presently standardized for the chemical constituents hypericin and pseudohypericin. All of the clinical studies performed with St. John's wort employed a standardized extract version. The raw herb was never used because its constituents cannot be guaranteed to exist at therapeutic levels—or to exist at all! When looking for hypericum, make sure to purchase the standardized extract.[1]

The subject of dosage can be confusing to consumers as well. In order to obtain the therapeutic results of the clinical studies, one needs to properly calculate the dosage of the over-the-counter hypericum products. If a standardized version of a tablet or capsule of hypericum contains 500 mg, then how many milligrams of total hypericin does it equal? What if the label says 250 mg? Fortunately, calculating the dosage of the standardized extract of hypericum is simple.

To calculate the standardized dosage of hypericin per tablet or capsule, multiply the dose in milligrams by the percentage of total hypericin. For example:

$$300 \text{ mg} \times 0.3\% \text{ hypericin} = 0.9 \text{ mg of hypericin}$$
$$500 \text{ mg} \times 0.2\% \text{ hypericin} = 1.0 \text{ mg of hypericin}$$

Once you know the amount of standardized total hypericin per tablet or capsule, you are ready to determine the amount of St. John's wort you will need per day to accomplish the desired effects. The number of doses per day can then be multiplied by this amount.

$$0.9 \text{ mg of hypericin} \times 3 \text{ doses} = 2.7 \text{ mg per day}$$
$$1.0 \text{ mg of hypericin} \times 2 \text{ doses} = 2.0 \text{ mg per day}$$

Recent clinical studies have not established an exact dose of St. John's wort extract that should be given to depressive or anxiety-ridden patients. Each of the studies, in fact, varied in the dosages administered of the herb. In some studies, patients were administered a dosage as low as 0.4 mg of hypericum extract per day; in other studies, patients were given doses as high as 2.7 mg hypericum extract per day. The European Scientific Corporation of Phytotherapy (ESCOP) recommends a dosage of 0.2 to

1.0 mg total hypericin per day.* However, this recommendation seems quite low and may not yield the most effective results.

Patients who exhibited the highest response rates in the clinical research studies used a dosage of 300 mg herbal extract three times per day, or 900 mg extract daily.[2] The percentage of those who responded to this dose was higher than those administered fewer milligrams of total hypericin per day (70 percent versus 60 percent). Most scientists and doctors have been recommending this daily dosage in accordance with medical supervision. The National Institutes of Health have also endorsed the 2.7 mg daily dosage. The U.S. multicenter trial of St. John's wort scheduled for 1998 will be using 300 mg tablets standardized to contain 0.3 percent hypericin by weight. Patients will receive the 300 mg tablet three times per day, a total of 2.7 mg. This amount is apparently the most commonly suggested of all the various doses. Of course, this dose is simply a recommended one, and can be adjusted according to the patient's needs.

Most of the products exhibited on the health food store shelves follow the recommendations of the clinical studies: 300 mg of St. John's wort standardized to contain 0.3 percent hypericin. Three tablets or capsules are suggested per day. It should be relatively easy to locate a St. John's wort product standardized to this amount since most companies consider this dosage appropriate based on current research and literature.

Capsules, Tablets, Extracts, and Tinctures

Tablets and capsules are very much alike. Both exist in the dry form, and both are equally effective in delivering the nutrients to the body. Encapsulated St. John's wort can be found in gelatin capsules and sometimes in vegicaps (capsules from a vegetable source). It is recommended that only the standardized version of hypericum be purchased in either of these forms to guarantee a high concentration of the active ingredient. Be sure to drink at least one cup of water per dose when taking capsules or tablets.

Standardized St. John's wort is also sold in tincture form. Sometimes

---

*ESCOP is a cooperative of various organizations involved in the development of therapeutic monographs. They have no regulatory weight, but carry authorative influence. They are based out of the University of Exeter, London.

tinctures are referred to as fluid extracts, however, they are two different entities. A tincture is a liquid preparation of herbs. Generally, the extraction process involves several steps. First, the herbs are ground. Next, they are extracted using alcohol or glycerin as a solvent. Sometimes an herb can sit in the solvent for as long as nine weeks before it is ready for preparation. Third and finally, the herb is pressed, and a tincture is created.

There are benefits and drawbacks to using this form of preparation. Unlike capsules and tablets, which take more time to disintegrate and ingest, fluid extracts largely bypass the digestive system and are assimilated into the bloodstream relatively quickly. On the flip side, it can be very difficult to determine exact dosage when administering the liquid. Unless there is a line on the dropper that indicates the specific amount to be taken per dose, or clear and precise directions on the label that instruct the number of drops per dose, self-dosing can be confusing. For this reason, some people like the convenience of a capsule or tablet. In addition, some people find the taste of St. John's wort objectionable. (I certainly do not find St. John's wort to be a bad tasting herb, but not everyone agrees.) Third, tinctures almost always contain alcohol. Alcohol is used in the extraction of the non-water-soluble compounds of the herb and as a preservative to maintain shelf life. Various persons may want to avoid the alcohol-based tinctures, such as children or those with blood sugar problems.

Unfortunately, capsules and tablets sometimes receive flak because they are not as easily assimilated by the body as extracts, but both are effective. Capsules, tablets, and tinctures are the only three forms that are sold in standardized forms, guaranteeing the exact level of active ingredient in every dose. Choosing between one and the other is a matter of choice, convenience, and cost.

Raw Herb

The raw crude version of hypericum can be purchased in bulk and as capsules and tablets. I did not discuss these versions of capsules or tablets in the section above because these are a nonstandardized version of the herb that has not been restructured or tampered with in any way. I have already discussed the drawbacks to using the raw dried hypericum in the treatment of depression, so I will add only a few points here. In any of the raw, dried forms, the active level of constituents probably vary. As a result, they cannot be guaranteed in each dose. Taking this version of the herb might not do much good for you because the active constituents may not be present in therapeutic amounts.

However, some herbalists prefer raw St. John's wort to the standardized preparation. Several systems of herbal health care, including Ayurvedic medicine, propose that the ingestion of the whole herb imparts an energy force that is compromised or eliminated during the standardization process. This school of thought sees herbs as more than the sum of their biochemical components. They are living forms capable of transmitting that energy (*prana* according to Ayurvedic medicine). For this reason, some herbalists or physicians may choose the raw version over the standardized extract or may skillfully combine the two. The whole form of the herb is thought to have a more complete metaphysical and biological effect on the user.

Tea and Oil

For hundreds of years, before the creation of standardized capsules, tablets, and extracts, people consumed St. John's wort as a tea for healing purposes. A few teaspoonfuls of the dried flowers and buds were added to a cup of boiling water, and the infusion was drunk. However, it probably required the consumption of fairly large amounts of the tea over an extended length of time (probably much longer than the two to six weeks that the standardized extract requires to take effect) to alter the spirits.

A tea prepared from St. John's wort can be taken in addition to the standardized extract without any ill effect on the daily dosage. Of course, let your physician know if you plan to drink more than one or two cups per day. While the tea is not standardized, it does contain unknown levels of the active ingredients. Additional cups of tea will elevate your dosage of hypericin, and this may or may not be such a good thing.

Oils made from hypericum are used mainly to speed the healing of wounds and skin irritations. Both St. John's wort oil and infusion have been used in the treatment of gastric conditions, including gastric ulcer and functional gastritis, nervous indigestion, and internal hemorrhoids.

The oil is also indicated for use in the treatment of inflammatory bowel syndrome. It is suggested to be administered as an overnight retention enema. The use of oils will be discussed in greater detail in the next chapter. Oils, however, are not useful in the treatment of depressive disorders.

One Tablet Three Times a Day? Or Three Tablets Once a Day?

Most people are following the suggested dosage of one tablet or capsule of St. John's wort three times per day with a meal. Taking hypericum at mealtime may offset any potential gastrointestinal disturbances that can occur if a supplement is taken on an empty stomach. One of the chief reasons persons experience stomach upset or nausea from medications or vitamins is because they are taken on an empty stomach. The stomach lining can become irritated when it is exposed to high concentrations of a medication. Few participants in the St. John's wort trials experienced stomach upset, but taking the extract at mealtime can keep this potential problem from erupting.

If your schedule makes it difficult to take one pill three times per day, two capsules or tablets can be taken in the morning with breakfast and one later in the midafternoon. This changed dosage should not interfere with the herbal medication's effects. As far as taking three capsules at once, I would not recommend it. The clinical studies have not researched this dosage and validated its efficacy. I doubt there are any serious health risks, but it is better to follow the same protocol successfully used by the scientists in the studies.

Incidentally, I have heard that a dose of St. John's wort extract (the terms *tincture* or *fluid extract* describe liquid preparation here, and *extract* is used when referring to the standardized extract of Hypericum available in capsule, tablet, and tincture form) near bedtime may result in insomnia for some users. I cannot comment on the validity of this claim, except to say that it is not uncommon to experience unexplained, idiosyncratic reactions to either drugs or herbal remedies. If you take the herb in the evening, and it does not adversely affect your sleep, then there is no reason not to take it at this time. If it ruins a good night's sleep, on the other hand, move the dose to the afternoon.

TABLE 2: ST. JOHN'S WORT DOSAGES*

The dosages of each form of hypericum vary and depend on the individual taking the remedy and the specific ailment being treated. Before attempting to self-medicate, you should seek the knowledgeable advice of a health practitioner. The dosages listed below are only meant to be guidelines.

Powder[†]	2 to 4 grams per day.
Infusion[†]	1 to 2 cups twice per day equal to 2 to 4 grams of the herb.
Tincture[†‡]	2 to 4 mL three times per day.
Fluid Extract (1:1)	Equal to 0.5 to 3.0 total hypericin per day.
Powdered Extract	Equal to 0.5 to 3.0 total hypericin per day.
Oil	1 teaspoon on an empty stomach when taken for gastric complaints, A.M. and P.M.

---

*Upton, R. et al. *American Herbal Pharmacopoeia and Therapeutic Compendium.* "St. John's wort: *Hypericum perforatum*." Santa Cruz, 1997.

[†]Or equivalent to 0.5 to 3.0 mg. of hypericin per day.

[‡]The extract strength range of 4:1 to 7:1 is suggested.

Lower Dose

The most effective dose of any medication is the minimum amount that yields the greatest effects with the fewest side effects. One cannot argue against such simplicity in pharmacotherapy. Fortunately for St. John's wort users, side effects are very rarely an issue with which patients need to contend. Establishing the correct dosage is probably the most difficult task in hypericum administration. Because there is no established dose at this time, dosages can be lowered or raised depending on the needs of the patient and the advice of the practitioner.

Some people feel uncomfortable about taking any medication—drug or herb—that has the potential to manipulate one's body and mind in any way. They might prefer to begin with a smaller amount of St. John's wort, perhaps 1.5 mg per day, roughly half of the suggested dose. While the higher dose is recommended more often and appears to act with greater effect, lower doses of hypericum have been effective on certain patients.

If after six weeks of treatment improvement is apparent, the dosage may be maintained or perhaps lowered. If the results are negligible, perhaps the dose should be raised.

Is More Better?

Normally, the effects of St. John's wort are gentle and gradual, and users may not notice changes in mood or behavior right away. It can take as many as six weeks for hypericum levels to reach steady-state concentrations in the body. This is a considerable length of time to wait if you are suffering from depression and anxiety. Thus, users of the herbal extract cite the long wait as a chief drawback in treatment.

Several scientists and doctors have postulated that initially higher doses of St. John's wort may solve this problem. Users may not need to wait so long if dosages of hypericum are elevated during the first several weeks of treatment, causing concentrations of hypericin to reach their steady state more quickly. Users may take as much as 10 mg of the herb daily or more in the beginning weeks of treatment of mild to moderate depression.[3] Later around the fourth to eighth week, once the effects of the herbal medication have been established, the dosage can be adjusted.

Higher doses of the herbal extract, more than 2.7 mg per day, may prove effective in the treatment of severe depressive disorder. High doses, taken over a long period of time, might be the missing link needed for successful treatment of severe depression with hypericum. Based on the past test results, it is ultimately conceivable that the herb could yield positive results. However, no research trials have investigated the influence of high doses on this type of depression.

SOLO OR COMBO?

St. John's wort has become such a popular herb that it is now included in almost every combination herbal stress supplement available on the market. Frequently, St. John's wort is offered with herbs such as valerian, hops, passion flower, and kava. Each one of these herbs is recognized as a nervine, thought to be capable of affecting the nervous system. Their combination with hypericum can be synergistic, adding to the quality of each herb and increasing the potential for each one's effects.

However, if you are looking to take St. John's wort at the same therapeutic dosage levels used in the clinical trials, then these combination herbal supplements are not for you. Combination supplements comprise several different herbs, each one present in small amounts. You might have to take several combination capsules to equal one standardized hypericum tablet or capsule. This is impractical and bothersome and could potentially be harmful, depending on the other herbs in the remedy. Stick to the standardized version of hypericum.

On the other hand, if you are not in need of the standardized extract of St. John's wort, you may find the multicomponent herbal formulas in this category effective.

SIDE EFFECTS

Several years ago, I came across a thought-provoking comment about side effects. There are no such things as side effects of a medication. There are only effects. Some effects are good and some effects are bad. The good effects are intended; the bad effects are unwanted, so they are called side effects.

This illustrates a good point. Often, we think of side effects as incidental or unrelated to the medicine's total mechanism of action. The spectrum of undesired effects is broad and ill defined. Sometimes the side effects of a medication are extremely threatening, outweighing the need for the remedy. Other times, they are trivial and do not pose any serious health risk.

St. John's wort's lack of side effects makes the herb a favorable option for those looking for an alternative to conventional drugs. None of the side effects associated with the herbal extract is appreciable. Numerous studies have been cited in which only small percentages of patients reported any side effects at all while taking the herb. In the 3,250-patient trial, only 2.4 percent of the patients involved experienced any side effects, and the actual numbers of patients who experienced them are very low. Intestinal symptoms were reported in 1 in 200; allergic reactions, 1 in 500; fatigue, 1 in 250; anxiety, 1 in 400; dizziness, less than 1 in 650; and miscellaneous reactions, less than 1 in 1,000. The observed incidence of side effects appears negligible.

When the percentages of patients who reported side effects in double-blind, placebo-controlled studies are added up, the number is only 4.1 percent. While the 4.1 percent is slightly higher than the 2.4 percent recorded in the 3,250-patient study, the number is significantly lower than the side effect response elicited from double-blind studies with conventional antidepressants. It is estimated that the average percentage of patients who experience side effects from hypericum treatment is roughly ten times less than those on conventional antidepressants. In addition, the therapy dropout rate is estimated at five times less.

The Placebo May Be Worse

In double-blind, placebo-controlled experiments, doctors do not expect patients in the placebo group to drop out of the study in greater numbers than the patients in the active substance group. Neither do they expect the former to report more side effects than the latter. But this unexpected turn of events is exactly what occurred in several professional hypericum trials. It stunned the scientists who reviewed the studies and the doctors who read about it.

A summary of fifteen studies performed on 1,008 patients recorded an ever so slight difference concerning the amount of side effects in the hypericum and placebo groups: 4.1 percent of the hypericum group recorded experiencing side effects versus 4.8 percent on the placebo. The dropout rates between the two were significantly more disparate: 0.4 percent of patients treated with hypericum left the studies early versus 1.6 percent of patients taking the placebo.[4] The number of "side effects" was more frequent in the placebo group than in the St. John's wort group![5]

To Avoid Side Effects

Fortunately, hypericum has so few potential side effects that physicians and patients need not worry a great deal about their development. In the event they do occur, however, then St. John's wort should be handled in the same manner as any other medication. The dosage of St. John's wort should be maintained at as high a level as necessary. A higher dose will insure a positive response. If a patient experiences particular side effects and is unable to tolerate them, the dose may be lowered. The side effects should disappear with time. If the side effects persist for any reason, one of two basic decisions can be made. The physician may opt to lower the dose, hoping that the lower dose will decrease the undesirable side effects without altering the herb's main effects, or the physician and patient may decide that the trade-off between symptom relief and side effects is satisfactory—the patient is receiving benefits from the herb, keeping the depression under control, and the side effects can be lived with.

Sometimes when medication levels are reduced from initial doses or when a medication is quit, side effects result. This tendency has not been noticed in the administration of St. John's wort. If hypericum is discontinued or the dosage is lowered, there is no reason side effects should appear. As explained earlier, the herb's slow rate of accumulation in the brain might be responsible for its benign side-effect profile.

Sensitive to the Sun

Another name for St. John's wort is Klamanth weed. Considered by some to be one of the peskiest weeds in the world, it grows wild throughout the United States, Canada, Europe, Asia, Africa, and Australia. St. John's wort thrives when left alone and prospers in damaged, hostile conditions—along roadsides, in rocky soil, fields that have been overgrazed by cattle, and construction sites. You have probably seen the so-called weed growing along the interstate at one time or another, but you may not have recognized it.

The herb that has been a blessing to those suffering from depression has been a curse to western ranchers. As kudzu has in the South, hypericum at one time invaded the entire Pacific Northwest. The herb took over ranch lands and pastures, growing everywhere. Cattle grazed heavily on the herb, and ranchers became obsessed with the necessity of its obliteration. They used herbicides to obliterate the herb, but when that method failed to work, the ranchers turned to an insect. They imported a beetle from Australia that possessed a ravenous appetite for the herb. Within ten years, the entire St. John's wort population was effectively reduced to 1 percent of its original numbers in the Pacific Northwest.[6]

Why were ranchers so obsessed with the herb's growth? They found that when cattle ate copious amounts of St. John's wort, they experienced a phototoxic reaction and often died from severe sunburn. Photoxicity is the increased, harmful sensitivity to sunlight. Chemicals in certain plants and synthetic medications can be activated in the skin by ultraviolet or visible radiation leading either to chemically induced photosensitivy reactions or to enhancement of the usual effects of sunlight.[7] There is a list of sixty to seventy prescription medications on the marketplace that can do this. Drugs such as tetracycline and sulfonamides are prime examples of photosensitizing agents. Although these medications are not likely to kill you if you are exposed to too much sun, they could cause a skin reaction with itching and redness.

Phototoxicity has never been noted in a single case of the treatment of depression with St. John's wort at recommended dosage levels. No death resulting from its use has ever been recorded in its 2,500 year history.

The reports of increased photosensitization in humans occurred in antiviral treatment of patients infected with HIV. Participants received intravenous injections of 35 mg of a synthetic hypericum extract. After twenty-four hours of exposure to sunlight, the worst symptoms recorded were rash and blistering sunburn. No long-term damage was experienced by those taking St. John's wort at these ultra-high doses.[8]

After years of widespread use, there have been no published reports of photosensitivity or phototoxicity of St. John's wort by the German Commission E. Scientists speculate that the chemical in hypericum capable of inducing photosensitivity might only do so at doses as high as 30 to 50 mg per day, dosages far beyond the recommended 2.7 mg per day. It is also thought that fair-skinned individuals are at higher risk for increased photosensitivity.

Don't worry about taking St. John's wort and visiting the beach or playing volleyball in the sun. The cattle and sheep that died ate large amounts of the herb every day, larger amounts than humans usually take. In addition, they persisted in eating the weed even after phototoxic reactions began to take place. If the dose is lowered or the medication is quit, photosensitivity disappears.

Interactions with Other Drugs

The use of several drugs is sometimes important to the successful treatment of an illness. Multiple drug therapy has become the norm in the treatment of depression, AIDS, high blood pressure, and other ailments. When a physician prescribes medications to be taken together, the doctor must know if the combination can result in an interaction.

When drugs interact with each other, the interaction may be beneficial, synergistically enhancing the effects of each medication, or the interaction may be adverse and lead to diminished or negative effects.[9]

It would be impossible to predict how every drug on the pharmaceutical market might react to St. John's wort. To do so would require research trials dedicated to observing the herb administered in combination with an exhaustive list of drugs. Test studies like this have not been performed on prescription medications. Instead, we predict how certain drugs may react to others based on their chemical components and on their behavior in test tube studies and animal models. Using humans in experimental trial would entail ethical implications that pharmaceutical companies are not eager to face.

At this point, scientists are largely unaware of which medications might interfere with St. John's wort. Unfortunately, like so many answers already given, this is a rather vague response. Yet this same response holds true to some degree for many drugs. Of chief importance to the use of St. John's wort in multidrug therapy are the potentially dangerous interactions with MAOIs. There are contraindications for using MAOIs in combination with St. John's wort because it is a suspected SSRI. You should also consult your physician before you combine the herb with Prozac or Paxil, both SSRI drugs. Too many chemicals influencing the inhibition of serotonin reuptake could possibly result in serotonin syndrome, causing agitation, sweating, and tremors. Before any possible drugs are discontinued or combined or any changes are made in treatment, it is essential to visit your physician.

Natural Supplements and St. John's Wort

After operating a homeopathic dispensary and health food store for quite some time, I know that people often adopt a "more is better" attitude. When treating a particular ailment, they take ten different remedies recommended for the treatment of that ailment. The assumption here is take everything natural and see what helps. This can be a potentially dangerous approach.

Herbs, vitamins, and other natural supplements are composed, like drugs, of particular chemicals that may have beneficial or adverse interactions. Systematic trials have never been performed to measure the effectiveness or safety of natural supplements in combination with one another, so caution and common sense should guide the St. John's wort user. Before you add any natural supplements to your program, it is suggested that you consult with your doctor.

CHILDREN TAKING HYPERICUM

Traditionally St. John's wort has been frequently recommended in the treatment of bed wetting in children, especially when the problem is due to nervous anxiety or nerve irritation in the bladder. However, there seems to be no general consensus among physicians about whether St. John's wort should be given to children. The chief reason for this is the lack of research; all of the clinical research trials performed up to date have included only adult subjects.

Dr. Jonathan Zeuss, author of *The Natural Prozac Program*, believes that children under twelve years of age should definitely not take St. John's wort. Citing children's different metabolisms and a lack of information about its safety and effectiveness in the treatment of clinical depression in children, Dr. Zeuss does not recommend the herb for them.[10] Dr. Steven Bratman, on the other hand, author of *Beat Depression with St. John's Wort*, reminds us that, although Prozac is frequently prescribed to children, clinical studies on Prozac were only performed with adult patients. On the basis of this reasoning, he contends that St. John's wort may be appropriate for children as well.[11]

While Dr. Bratman's assumption that hypericum is safe for children might be correct, his reasoning leaves something to be desired. He does, however, make an interesting point about Prozac. Why are children given Prozac if there is no clinical evidence to document its safety for children? I do not have an answer except to say perhaps it should not be.

Physicians who administer St. John's wort to children are cautious about doing so, and parents should not give the herb to their children without a doctor's advice. One of the most common formulas to calculate a child's daily dose is Clark's rule: the child's weight is divided by 150 pounds, the average adult weight; the resulting number is multiplied by the average adult dosage (2.7 mg). The answer is the recommended child's daily dose.

PREGNANT OR NURSING WOMEN

There is no scientific evidence addressing the use of St. John's wort by women who are pregnant or nursing. The herb may temporarily reduce the production of breast milk during lactation, but this action has not been confirmed or contradicted. When pregnant or nursing, it may be better to avoid hypericum in light of insufficient data.

CHAPTER 6

HEALING HYPERICUM

For thousands of years, traditional herbalists have not limited the use of St. John's wort to its effect on the emotions and the brain. It has been widely used in the treatment of a variety of physiological disorders. Its most original and fundamental role in the healing process includes its employment as a natural antibiotic, wound healer, antiviral, cancer fighter, anti-inflammatory, and pain reliever. Additionally, the herb has potent cardiovascular effects and is useful in the treatment of chronic tension headaches. Today, St. John's wort continues to be prescribed for these purposes, and science now confirms the various medicinal uses of St. John's wort previously recorded by folk healers.

Unlike single entity drugs, which tend to focus on one particular action, hypericum has many actions. This is difficult to understand in light of our present knowledge of drugs and their lone mechanisms of action. It is an entirely peculiar concept that an herb is capable of affecting the physical body in such comprehensive ways. Put simply, herbs are not isolated, chemically defined substances. Many different chemicals exist within the roots, leaves, stems, or flowers, and thus the range of action of a particular herb is multiplicitous, with each chemical influencing the body in a specific and distinct way.

Although hypericum comprises numerous chemical compounds and has several pharmacological effects, it would be a mistake to think of the herb as unique or superior to other herbs in this respect. In fact, all herbs possess multiple actions and can have beneficial effects on more than one condition. Any reader browsing through a medicinal herbal for the first time may be surprised by an herb's long list of clinical applications. The sheer number of therapeutic effects may seem highly implausible or incredulous to the herbal neophyte. For example, clinical studies performed on garlic show that the immune-enhancing herb is effective in the treatment of numerous conditions, including high blood pressure and high cholesterol, and has antifungal, antiviral, and anticancer activities. Likewise, some of the clinical applications of hypericum may sound improbably fantastic at times, but the clinical evidence is present. Hypericum is good for other things besides depression.

THE FOREIGN INVADERS

They are liable to visit at any time, from anywhere. Maybe they are lurking on the door to the restroom at your favorite restaurant, or on a library book shared by hundreds of other readers, or in the sneeze of a passerby on the busy streets of the city. It could even be the benign lick of your beloved dog happy to see you return home at the end of a long day. No matter where you turn, pests like viruses and bacteria are out there. Even though you may not see them, they are not hiding from you. Unafraid and unabashed, these microscopic critters are at work daily in a world our eyes cannot penetrate. They invade the body and attempt to make their homes there. Some are harmless, but others, as we well know, are carriers of sometimes deadly diseases.

Years ago, with the discovery of antibiotics, scientists thought the fight against bacteria was over and they were beginning to turn their attention to cancers and viruses. But bacteria were a little smarter than their considerably larger opponents and they became resistant to the drugs the doctors gave. Scientists attempted to modify the antibiotics and stay one step ahead of the microorganisms, but their methods no longer worked as successfully. Researchers continue to search for new ways to dupe the pathogens at their own game.

NO VIRUSES ACCEPTED HERE

Perhaps the herb with yellow flowers will be the secret weapon of choice in the battle against deadly viruses next. Researchers have already demonstrated that St. John's wort possesses significant antiviral activity. St.

John's wort has been shown to be quite effective against a wide variety of lipid-enveloped, or encapsulated, viruses that include the herpes simplex virus (both types 1 and 2, the causes of cold sores and genital herpes), flu virus, hepatitis C, and HIV.[1, 2] The herb has also exhibited significant influence over the Epstein-Barr virus, the same virus responsible for infectious mononucleosis and sometimes present in Chronic Fatigue Syndrome. It also has been shown to be effective in the treatment of vesicular stomatitis virus.[3] These studies have shown that two active components of hypericum, hypericin and psuedohypericin, yield the impressive antiviral activity.

Currently, clinical trials are under way in the United States to investigate the antiviral activity of hypericin. To date, all of the research performed with St. John's wort in the treatment of viruses has used a purified, synthetic form of hypericin. It was necessary for researchers to create a synthesized version of the compound because experiments require much higher doses of hypericin than any plant extract can yield. The natural version of hypericin exists at remarkably low levels in the actual plant, less than 1 percent of the whole herb.[4]

USING HYPERICIN IN AIDS TREATMENT

In 1988 a study published in the *Proceedings of the National Academy of Sciences* created a great deal of interest in the use of St. John's wort as a treatment for HIV/AIDS.[5] The article reported that researchers at New York University Medical Center and the Weizmann Institute of Science in Israel demonstrated the anti-retroviral activity of hypericin and pseudohypericin. Preliminary studies investigated the effects of the synthetic form of the two compounds in the treatment of the Friend leukemia virus and the radiation leukemia virus, both viruses that are highly similar to HIV. The test was carried out in test tubes and on mice (in vitro and in vivo).

Researchers concluded that the two compounds show great promise in the treatment of HIV, the virus responsible for AIDS. Mice infected with the retrovirus were administered a single, relatively small dose of hypericin and pseudohypericin. The effects of the medicine on the mice were dramatic, both in its mechanism of action and because of its seemingly small potency. The onset of disease and death was slowed down considerably in the animals. Interestingly, the results of the test were equivalent whether the compounds were administered orally or intravenously.

The medicinal compound appeared to operate in two distinct ways. First, the activation process of the virus itself was impeded. Second, hypericin situated itself on cellular membranes and offered protection against the viruses' attack. The herb's penetration of the blood-brain barrier is also important in the treatment of the virus because the virus normally attacks the brain. No pharmacological drug is capable of performing the exact function of the hypericin compound; its mechanism of action is truly exceptional and unique.

After the success of the mouse studies had been established, and news had spread that hypericin appeared to be an effective treatment in Friend leukemia, AIDS researchers became interested in the compound. They were anxious to see how it would affect human patients suffering from the disease. In 1991 three medical centers in the United States ran federally sponsored clinical trials. Patients were administered hypericin intravenously at roughly ten times the normal daily dose twice per week. Some patients recorded improvement, but unfortunately, many needed to withdraw from the studies because the phototoxic side effects induced by the synthetic hypericin were too uncomfortable for some of the patients to bear. In test tubes, however, early laboratory work has already demonstrated healthy T-lymphocyte cells that are resistant to infection by HIV, so it seems as though hypericin inactivates the virus and protects the cells from attack.[6]

I am not aware of any subsequent federally sponsored clinical trials, but I know of several private trials that are currently being conducted. In the Phoenix metropolitan area, Dr. Alan Christianson is participating in a regional research study. His patients have all been diagnosed with AIDS and all are receiving 10 mg per day of the natural, standardized extract, administered orally. So far, one-half of the patients have experienced a substantial decrease in total viral load, approximately 40 percent, according to Dr. Christianson. He has also recorded changes in general symptoms, which include an improvement in immune function and appetite and increase in energy. Karposi sarcoma lesions also gradually became smaller.

More studies are needed before we will know whether or not hypericin is effective in the treatment of AIDS. The side effects of hypericin may be a significant impediment to achieving the therapeutic action of the compound. The doctors had to limit their patients' dosages, thus losing the opportunity to determine the extract's therapeutic effects at higher doses.

Ironically, the antiviral activity of hypericun appears to depend on light. The same phototoxicity that proves fatal to cows may potentially aid humans on their road to recovery. When hypericin is exposed to light, through the skin in which it is absorbed into the tissues, its activity is multiplied. Investigators are not sure whether or not sun exposure may improve the response of AIDS patients taking hypericin. The photosensitizing reaction leaves researchers with many questions. They are now working on methods to minimize this reaction through possible combinations with other extracts in order to still yield its positive effects, but lessen the potential for photosensitiviy. (In the sun these patients sunburn extremely easily.)

Scientists certainly hope that hypericin will be effective in the treatment of AIDS some day, alone or as part of a drug cocktail, with the other medicines currently being prescribed for sufferers of the disease. As additional research is completed, scientists may be able to define the role hypericin plays in the treatment of HIV.

BLOOD CLEANERS

Several investigators who contributed to the research on hypericin and AIDS are spearheading new studies on the use of hypericin to prevent the spread of viruses through blood transfusions. The medicinal compound hypericin was added directly to units of blood intentionally contaminated with HIV. Then the blood was illuminated with a fluorescent light for a period of time. Investigators found that hypericin totally inactivated the viruses present in the blood. While blood is already screened before it is used for transfusion, the potential antiviral implications of hypericin are enormous. Sometimes, infectious agents find a way to slither past the screening test process, and the addition of hypericin to units of blood may prevent this from happening.

One particular virus that has been practically impossible to beat is hepatitis C. Like certain other infectious agents, it is commonly spread through blood transfusions. This form of hepatitis is a serious one and can potentially cause severe liver damage or even liver cancer in individuals.

It is estimated that 150,000 individuals in the United States are diagnosed with this form of hepatitis every year. Several medical centers in
New York are now experimenting with hypericin for this purpose, and
preliminary studies look promising.

THE WOUND HEALER

Herbalists have long recognized St. John's wort as a potent wound
healer. Throughout history soldiers in the battlefield have also valued its
wound-healing effects. The knights of St. John of Jerusalem used the
herb as did the soldiers who fought during the U.S. Civil War. But St.
John's wort's uses have not been limited to physical injuries incurred on
battlefields. Animal and snake bites, bruises, burns, hemorrhoids, ulcer-
ations, eczema, psoriasis, sunburn, frost bite, and other skin problems
have also been treated successfully with St. John's wort.

Preparing the plant for use in the treatment of wounds is a simple
process. After the fresh leaves and flowers are collected, they are finely
chopped, steeped in vegetable oil for a month or two and then strained.
It is important to expose the oil to sunlight while it steeps, allowing it
to sit on a windowsill or in any other location where it will be exposed
to ample amounts of sunlight. In several weeks, the oil turns red in color,
from the hypericin's exposure to the sun. This preparation has traditionally been used as an ointment for many different skin inflammations.[7]
Sometimes St. John's wort oil is prepared from the fresh flowers alone.
After they are picked, they are stored in olive or soybean oil for several
weeks. The flowers are strained, and the oil is ready to use.[8]

Researchers have been very impressed by hypericum's success in the
treatment of wounds. In 1975 researchers prepared a burn ointment
from the fresh flowers. They mixed 5 mg of the fresh flowers with 100
grams of olive oil and allowed the solution to sit for ten days at room
temperature. Scientists watched with intense interest research that demonstrated the wound-healing effects of the plant.

The first-degree burns treated with hypericum ointment healed within
forty-eight hours of application. The second- and third-degree burns
showed a remarkably quick response to the ointment, healing at least
three times more quickly than burns treated with conventional treatments, such as colloid gels and other topical agents like alantoin or
iodine swabs to stave off infections. The hypericum ointment inhibited

keloid formation, or the growing scar tissue formed after a burn or other injury.[9]

One newsworthy study conducted by researchers compared the wound-healing powers of St. John's wort to those of calendula, an herb considered by many to be the ruler of healing herbs. The hypericum was administered orally while the calendula was used topically. The effects of hypericum were found to be more definitive than those of the calendula tincture. The topical application of calendula is well known and standard practice among herbalists. The fact that the internal use of St. John's wort proved more effective in treatment than the topical application of calendula is well noted. People in the industry will be surprised to learn of St. John's wort's potent wound-healing properties. Without dismissing the virtues of calendula, researchers believe St. John's wort deserves to share the spotlight.

NATURE'S ANTIBIOTIC

Hypericum's success as a potent wound healer seems to be due in part to its function as a natural antibiotic. Several components of the St. John's wort plant contribute to this antibiotic action—the essential oil, the phloroglucinols, and the flavonoids. It is thought that the essential oil has minor antifungal and significant broad-spectrum antimicrobial activity. In one research paper, it was reported that an extract of the plant was found to be effective against gram-positive bacteria. Other studies have shown that it is equally effective against gram-negative bacteria.[10]

Other components of the plant, the tannins and flavonoids, were useful against *E. coli (Escherichia coli)*, the bacterium most often responsible for urinary tract infections. These components were tested against the bacteria in relatively high dilutions and successfully deactivated the bacteria.[11] As a result of these studies, some naturopathic doctors are recommending the use of the tincture to prevent urinary tract infections, which are common among women.

Nicholas Culpeper, a famed herbalist, recommended that St. John's wort be used for "spitting blood," a common symptom of tuberculosis, the once deadly disease still responsible for three million deaths per year.[12] The plant has been recommended against the *Staphylococcus aureus* infection, too. While the staph bacteria normally live in the body without causing any problems, anytime an injury or wound is introduced to the body the bacteria can make its presence known. Thus, hospitals are especially wary of staph infections.

Other microorganisms affected by St. John's wort include *Candida albicans, Proteus vulgaris, Pseudomonas aeruginosa,* and *Streptococcus mutans.*[13, 14] Besides hypericum's direct antimicrobial effect, the herb is effective in enhancing overall immune function. This action contributes to the defeat of the various killer microbes by the medicinal herb.

NATURE'S ANTI-INFLAMMATORY

Whether the herb is taken as a tincture or applied topically as an ointment, the use of St. John's wort as an anti-inflammatory is unparalleled. Historically, it has been employed extensively as a medicine in the treatment of nerve pain and inflammation. Any sign of nerve irritation is a definite call for this herb. Dr. M. L. Tyler, author of *Homeopathic Drug Pictures,* offers an excellent, concise description of the principal use of the plant, while extolling its benefits. He writes, "Among the Wound-worts and Bruise-worts of our land, none rivals Hypericum for its healing touch on injured nerves, and for injuries—especially to parts rich in nerves. Here we use it both externally and internally."[15]

His unbridled enthusiasm for the plant has good reason. St. John's wort is currently being recommended in the treatment of various disorders, including neuralgia, or pain from a damaged nerve; trigeminal neuralgia, a specific form of neuralgia affecting the trigeminal nerve, the major nerve in the face (also known as tic douloureux); and sciatica, the pain caused by pressure on the sciatic nerve, the largest of all nerves with branches that run throughout the lower body and legs.[16] Daily local application of the ointment and oral use of the extract are suggested. An infusion of St. John's wort is recommended as a mouthwash and gargle for mouth pain.

HOMEOPATHIC ST. JOHN'S WORT

St. John's wort's reputation as an anti-inflammatory is well known in a branch of natural medicine called homeopathy, a two-hundred-year-old system of healing. The word *homeopathy* is derived from the Greek words for "similar suffering." Homeopathy is based on the principle that "like cures like." Homeopathic remedies consist of minute amounts of plant extracts and other natural substances that, in large doses, cause the symptoms being experienced. Homeopathy finds solutions to different ailments through a wide range of natural substances derived from different parts of the world, including the ocean, the forest, and the desert. Different natural substances from minerals to insects are utilized—even various poisons such as snake and bee venom are included in the homeopathic arsenal of medications.[17]

Unlike standard prescription drugs and herbal supplements, these medicines are prepared according to the science of homeopathic pharmacology. Potentization, the pharmaceutical process used, involves successive dilution and succussion of the remedies. Potentization is thought to keep toxic properties to a minimum while increasing the medicines' potential to cure.

The homeopathic preparation of St. John's wort is referred to as Hypericum (all homeopathic medicines are identified by their Latin nomenclature). Although homeopathic medicines are different from the typical herbal extracts sold in stores, the therapeutic uses of the homeopathic tincture are consistent with the therapeutic uses in modern herbal therapy.[18] The homeopathic tincture is similar to the liquid extract. The tincture has not been patented—it is simply a concentrated alcohol solution provided. The original substance is soluble in alcohol.

Homeopaths prescribe the herb to relieve pain and inflammation of nerve origin, including the painful extraction of a tooth, shingles, chronic nerve pain from bone fractures, spinal injuries, musculoskeletal trauma, and surgical trauma. Other indications for the use of St. John's wort include burning or tingling pain, and twitching or spasms, as a result of any traumatic nerve injuries such as cuts or burns.[19]

THE CANCER WARRIOR

Several research studies have suggested that St. John's wort might hold promise as a cancer treatment. The Trinity Medical Center in North Dakota is currently performing research on hypericin and its use in the treatment of glioma, a common and deadly form of brain cancer. Severely ill patients who have not responded to conventional cancer treatment are participating in the study, which is spearheaded by neurosurgeon Dr. William Couldwell. The study is not over yet, but so far the results of hypericin treatment look encouraging.[20]

Hypericin's antiglioma effects appear to equal or even surpass the effects of Tamoxifen, one of the most widely used cancer chemotherapy medications. In the study, hypericin did not require light to activate its anticancer activity, but the presence of light increased anticancer activity. Unlike the AIDS trials, the doses were low enough that the researchers did not see any photosensitizing reactions. It should be mentioned that, as in the AIDS trials, a purified, synthetic form of hypericin was employed.

This research has spurred additional studies in the field. Researchers at UCLA are undertaking these studies on the use of hypericin in the treatment of other forms of cancer, including melanoma and breast cancer.

Another incredible discovery worthy of mention is the news that the standardized extract of St. John's wort may help prevent cancer. One published study showed that the extract exerts an antimutagenic effect on cells, preventing cells from becoming cancerous.[21, 22]

ENHANCED BLOOD FLOW

Research studies have shown that in addition to hypericum's antidepressant and antiviral effects, St. John's wort is beneficial to the cardiovascular system. One particular study involved guinea pig hearts. The herb was found to be clinically effective in enhancing the flow of blood through coronary blood vessels, the vessels that supply the heart with essential oxygen and nutrients. The effects of the herb are due to its constituent procyanidin, the same flavonoid compound responsible for hawthorn's *(Crataegus oxyacantha)* beneficial cardiovascular effects. Naturopathic doctors, incidentally, frequently recommend hawthorn for diseases affecting the cardiovascular system.

The same researchers who examined the benefits of the procyanidins in hypericum made another surprising discovery. The procyanidin factions were found to disrupt the action of histamine and prostaglandin F, two chemicals known for their potential to cause constriction of the arteries. It certainly appears that procyanidin is very effective in its influence over coronary blood flow.[23]

WEIGHT LOSS

Since St. John's wort has become the talk of the town, it has been included in a number of multiherb combinations promoted as weight loss aids. Although there is no clinical evidence that St. John's wort is capable of accelerating the fat burning process and controlling metabolism, some manufacturers are capitalizing on the herb's alleged effects on serotonin to promote it as a weight loss supplement.

Depression is often accompanied by increased cravings for simple carbohydrates and weight gain. Lower levels of serotonin are thought to be responsible for this secondary symptom. On the basis of this knowledge, it is theorized that hunger, or more specifically, the craving for carbohydrates, may be triggered or altered by low serotonin levels. Because St. John's wort is thought to increase serotonin levels it may reduce certain food cravings.

Remember Fen-phen, the popular drug that was removed from the market in September 1997 because of its negative cardiovascular effects? Fen-phen was actually a mixture of two drugs (phentermine, a stimulant, and fenfluramine, pondimin) credited with boosting serotonin levels. Apparently, chemicals that affect the serotonin pathway play a role in weight reduction.

Before purchasing any diet products, it is a good idea to consult someone who is familiar with dietary supplements. There may be fifty different products on the shelf to choose from, each formula a little bit different than the other. Certain supplements contain ingredients whose use might be contraindicated in various conditions.

CHAPTER 7

OTHER NATURAL TREATMENTS
FOR DEPRESSION

The practice of medicine is an art rather than a science.
Most of the treatments that doctors prescribe every day are
no more "proven" than the alternative methods they criti-
cize. Accepting unproven and dangerous treatments, while
rejecting safer and less expensive natural alternatives, is a
bizarre double standard.

Alan R. Gaby, M.D.

This chapter examines natural alternatives to prescription drugs that are
widely used in the treatment of depression and anxiety. These include
such herbs as kava and *Ginkgo biloba,* as well as a variety of amino acids,
essential fatty acids, vitamins, and homeopathic medications. Whether
these nutraceuticals are used alone, or in combination with one another,
they continue to show great promise in treatment. Their concomitant
effectiveness and benign side-effect profile have made these supplements favorites—and their popularity is on the rise—among both the
general public and naturopathic physicians. Like St. John's wort, these
remedies may become the "natural superpowers" of the future—indeed,
a few already have. Easy to locate, these remedies are widely distributed
throughout the health food industry via health stores, pharmacies, and
natural co-ops.

KAVA

The February 26, 1998 issue of the *Wall Street Journal* featured an article on the herb kava, calling it the latest herb to make a splash with powerful health claims. "Today, thanks to behind-the-scenes promoting by Mr. Kilham (author of *Kava: Medicine Hunting in Paradise*) and a cadre of other devotees," writes Andrea Petersen, author of the article, "kava is poised to become the next blockbuster herbal remedy. For the millions who bought Ginkgo biloba to sharpen their memory and St. John's wort to treat depression, kava is being pitched as a natural way to heal another big modern woe: anxiety."[1]

Dubbed the "Pacific elixir," kava has been widely used by South Pacific societies, including those in Melanesia, Polynesia (including Somoa and Tonga), and Micronesia for thousands of years. There, where swaying palm trees, volcanoes, and sandy beaches are home to warm tropical weather, kava grows all over the islands. A member of the pepper family (*Piper methysticum* of the *Piperaceae*, a cultivated kava), its name means "intoxicating pepper." A slow-growing, but erect and well-branching perennial, it is an attractive shrub that on average reaches a height of 2 to 2.5 meters, although under certain conditions it may reach a height of 6 meters. The stump of the shrub, commonly referred to as the rootstock, is home to the active pharmacological compounds that are responsible for its mood altering effects. The compounds—actively referred to as *kavalactones*—include *kavain, methysticin, dihydrokavin,* and *dihydromethysticin*.[2] Several additional studies have concluded that the above ground portions of the plant contain high concentrations of compounds that are also responsible for its relaxant properties.

The Traditional Herb

Kava is a favorite among the locals in these societies, used for its psychoactive properties, and appreciated for its rich history. It is said among South Pacific drinkers of kava that the herb inspires friendship and that it is impossible to feel hatred once the herb has been drunk. Taken by islanders for more than three thousand years, the first encounter with kava by Europeans was during the first exploratory voyage of Captain James Cook (1768–1771). George Forester, a young naturalist who sailed with Cook on the first voyage, is credited with giving the plant its name and the first description of its use. He witnessed two

Polynesians prepare and drink the kava:

> [Kava] is made in the most distgustful manner that can be imagined from the juice contained in the roots of a species of pepper-tree. This root is cut small, and the pieces chewed by several people, who spit the macerated mass into a bowl, where some water (milk) of coconuts is poured upon it. They then strain it through a quantity of the fibres of coconuts, squeezing the chips, till all their juices mix with the coconut-milk; and the whole liquor is decanted into another bowl. They swallow this nauseous stuff as fast as possible; and some old toppers value themselves on being able to empty a great number of bowls.[3]

Chewing the kava root is no longer part of the preparation process—a practice that over time ended in most of the Pacific islands, with the exception of the southern islands of Vanuatu and parts of Papua New Guinea. Interestingly, the chewing of the root is not as repugnant as one might think contrary to what many European and American explorers and missionaries originally conjectured, the practice was not born out of barbarism and the unhygienic nature of the natives, but simply because they believed that chewing the root produced a more potent drink. Scientific investigation does reveal that mastication liberates the active components in the root, because the saliva contains an enzyme that breaks down the starchy components of the pulp.[4]

From an anthropological standpoint kava is a unique herb in that it has played an integral role in the religious, economic, political, and social life of the Pacific inhabitants. Traditionally it has been employed in cultural and religious ceremonies as a means toward achieving higher consciousness, greater perception, and spiritual inspiration. In these cultures the drinking of kava signals good friendship and is shared between leaders and followers, friends and equals, even prime ministers and voters. New relations with strangers are created by sharing kava because it evokes feelings of camaraderie and mutual understanding. Poor relations between people are often repaired with the use of kava.

Kava has been seen as an "important traditional exchange item that also links people with their gods and ancestral spirits."[5] The use of kava in religious ceremonies differs from the traditional employment of sacraments in the Christian tradition. In native religions the drinking of kava produces altered states of consciousness that function as doors of perception to the supernatural realm. In this world, kava is an important means of inspiration and inner wisdom.[6] It is believed that the spirits of ancestors speak to people in altered states of consciousness, therefore, persons intoxicated with kava can converse with the dead. Those who take part in the kava ceremony, a ritual practiced among the islanders, are "transported to the realm of ancestors and gods." The kava root is also used as an object of sacrifice.

A more recent—and one of the most definitive—descriptions of kava intoxication is given by researcher R. J. Gregory after he tried the libation:

> Kava seizes one's mind. This is not a literal seizure, but something does change in the processes by which information enters, is retrieved, or leads to actions as a result. Thinking is certainly affected by the kava experience, but not in the same ways as are found from caffeine, nicotine, alcohol, or marijuana. I would personally characterize the changes I experienced as going from lineal processing of information to a greater sense of "being" and contentment with being. Memory seemed to be enhanced, whereas restriction of data inputs was strongly desired, especially with regard to disturbances of light, movements, noise, and so on. Peace and quiet were very important to maintain the inner sense of serenity. My senses seemed to be unusually sharpened, so that even whispers seemed to be loud while loud noises were extremely unpleasant.[7]

A kava-induced state of mild euphoria and reduced anxiety has made kava a popular herb around the world—especially among herb users looking for natural alternatives to drugs. Research on kava has focused on its use as a relaxant, although kava possesses antidepressant, antianxiety, and soporific properties as well. It is also an excellent tranquilizing herb, and "a first-rate sedative, producing calm and promoting sleep if taken in sufficient quantity."[8]

Clinical Research

In the European pharmaceutical market, kava is sold for nervous disorders, sleep disorders, psychiatric disorders, anxiety, tension, and restlessness.[8] In the United States, kava is gaining popularity as a sleep aid and anxiolytic. Like St. John's wort, it is prepared as an extract standardized for kavalactone content—30 to 70 percent. The typical dosage is 45 mg–75 mg of extract containing 30 percent kavalactones with a daily dosage of 1 to 3 capsules. More may be taken at bedtime to promote good sleep.

A study published in the journal *Pharmopsychiatry* followed 101 patients suffering from anxiety of nonpsychotic origin for twenty-five weeks in a multicenter trial randomized placebo-controlled and double-blind study utilizing the kava extract. According to the Hamilton Anxiety Scale (HAMA), kava was found to be significantly superior to the placebo by week eight. Researchers further concluded that the herbal extract is a suitable alternative to the standard tricyclics prescribed in the treatment of depression and to the benzodiazapines used in the treatment of various anxiety disorders.[9]

Another double-blind study also verified the clinical effectiveness of kava. Thirty-eight patients were given either a kava extract or oxazepam, a drug similar to Valium, for four weeks. While both groups demonstrated improvement according to their anxiety scores (Self-Rating Anxiety Scale and Anxiety Status Inventory), kava was found to be nonaddictive and free of side effects, unlike oxazepam and similar drugs that are well known for dangerously addictive qualities.[10]

Another study involved menopause in women—a period in a woman's life that can be marked by increased nervousness and anxiety. The eight-week trial was double-blind and studied forty women. One hundred mg of kava extract standardized for 70 percent kavalactones or placebo were administered 1 to 3 times per day. According to the HAMA, after one week, there were significant improvements in the kava group. As the trial continued, the beneficial effects in the kava group became more pronounced. The researchers recorded improvements in both general mood and menopausal symptoms, including hot flashes, among those participants taking kava.[11]

Conclusion

Clinical researchers have concluded that kava extract is beneficial in the treatment of anxiety and depression. Its natural mood elevating, stress reducing, and other anxiolytic properties establish it as an effective replacement for addictive benzodiazapines. The contraindications for its use are few: primarily individuals affected by Parkinson's disease should abstain from using kava. While long-term overuse of the herb in large quantities can cause dry, scaly skin, suggested daily dosages do not cause such reactions. Because of its few drawbacks, it is likely we will see this herb become increasingly popular over the next several years, joining the ranks of other herbal superstars such as St. John's wort, Ginkgo biloba, and echinacea.

5-HTP

Earlier in the book, we discussed the importance of the neurotransmitter serotonin. In a January 1998 issue of *Newsweek,* a timely article about serotonin was released that investigated its role in human health and well-being. "As the twentieth century winds down," the authors reported, "we humans seem increasingly convinced that serotonin is the key to a good life—and it's easy to see why. This once obscure neurotransmitter is the secret behind Prozac, the drug that revolutionized the pursuit of happiness 10 years ago this winter. Prozac and its mood-altering cousins all work by boosting serotonin's activity in the brain. So do Redux and fenfuramine, the blockbuster diet drugs that were pulled off the market this fall due to safety concerns. Even Imitrex, the hot new migraine treatment, works it magic via serotonin. Somehow serotonin is implicated in just about everything that matters to us—from winning friends and wielding power to managing anxiety and controlling appetites and impulses."[12]

Many health food store patrons are coming into contact with a relatively new product that, like St. John's wort, is being hailed as the latest natural wonder cure. Basically it is a new form of *tryptophan* called *L-5-hydroxytryptophan,* or *5-HTP* for short. L-tryptophan and its derivative 5-HTP are both precursors to serotonin. Because serotonin cannot cross the blood-brain barrier, the brain must produce its own serotonin supply, and production of this specific neurotransmitter in the brain requires the uptake of the amino acid tryptophan. The word *tryptophan* is recognizable to many people as a popular amino acid that was taken for quite some time to keep the brain adequately supplied with serotonin. Since the early 1990s, however, sales of this product have been banned. The controversy surrounding its ban is strong although the reasons for the ban remain somewhat elusive.

A naturally occurring amino acid, tryptophan is required for the production of melatonin and serotonin, two neurohormones involved in mood and sleep regulation. Clinical studies on serotonin show that it plays an important role in supporting feelings of well-being, calmness, relaxation, concentration, confidence, and security. A deficiency of this neurotransmitter may be the pivotal factor in the development of depression, sleep disorders, obesity, and addiction.[13] 5-HTP has been a godsend to those people who have been unable to legally obtain L-tryptophan for the last several years.

L-Tryptophan

For years L-tryptophan was commonly used for pain control, anxiety, depression, PMS, various manic-depressive and obsessive-compulsive disorders, and sleep problems.[14] But in November 1989 the FDA pulled the amino acid off the market and in March of 1990 banned its sale and distribution following reports of more than fifteen hundred cases of Eosinophilia-Myalgia Syndrome (EMS) and twenty-seven deaths related to the use of tyrptophan-containing supplements. EMS is a potentially fatal blood disease commonly associated with parasitic infections or severe allergies.[15] Researchers at the Centers for Disease Control (CDC) released an FDA commissioned report in August 1992, however, that certifiably cleared tryptophan as the cause of the EMS outbreak. The research was conducted by the CDC, the Mayo Clinic, the Oregon State Health Division, and the Minnesota Department of Health and reported that virtually all cases of EMS related to L-tryptophan were traced to contaminants found in batches of tryptophan manufactured by a single Japanese petrochemical firm, Showa Denko. Of six Japanese companies that supplied tryptophan to the United States, Showa Denko was the source for 60 percent of the country's supply. The contaminants resulted from changes made in the manufacturing procedures, and this direct cause-and-effect relationship was documented and released in the November 1990 *Journal of Clinical Investigation*.

Prior to the EMS epidemic, the amino acid had enjoyed an outstanding safety record and, therefore, it was assumed by many in the health food industry that after its exoneration tryptophan supplements would soon return to store shelves. But this was not to be the case. Seemingly unfairly, the amino acid was banned from the market, and as of this winter the FDA has revealed no plans to lift the ban of its sales. Other countries rescinded their ban once the amino acid had been cleared of charges (in the United States L-tryptophan has been sanctioned for sale for animal use, but not for human use). In the meanwhile, an even more effective amino acid may have emerged: 5-HTP.

5-HTP is considered a safer alternative to the supplement L-tryptophan. Unlike tryptophan, it is not produced by chemical synthesis or bacterial formation. Instead it is extracted from the seed of the Griffonia plant, a source of commonly used pharmaceutical grade compounds, which decreases the risk of the contamination associated with the production of 5-HTP, thus avoiding a crisis similar to the EMS episode.

5-HTP and Depression

5-HTP has been undergoing research for over twenty-five years. One six-week study of sixty-nine subjects compared the use of 5-HTP to Luvox, a standard SSRI; both compounds were found to have equal antidepressant capabilities. But those who were administered the extract of the Griffonia plant experienced only half as many moderate-to-severe side effects as the prescription drug group. Like St. John's wort, 5-HTP seems to have fewer adverse effects than the prescription drugs used in the treatment of the same conditions.

Another study showed that 5-HTP had substantial stimulatory effects. A 200 mg daily dose increased endorphin levels in subjects suffering from major depression,[16] and many other studies document its effectiveness in elevating brain serotonin. Most researchers feel that 5-HTP is the safest tryptophan available. And it is ten times more effective than L-tryptophan in that a 50 mg dose of 5-HTP is comparable to a 500 mg dose of L-tryptophan. The suggested dose is 50–100 mg per day, although some doctors suggest dosages significantly beyond that amount. Vitamin B_6 supplementation is recommended while being administered 5-HTP, because it is a cofactor for the enzyme responsible for degrading toxic tryptophan metabolites; it is required for the enzymatic conversion of 5-HTP into serotonin. The use of vitamin B_3 (niacinimide) has also shown to be helpful used in conjunction with 5-HTP because it increases brain tryptophan levels. 5-HTP supplements usually contain both.

Contraindications

5-HTP should not be taken by individuals who are already on SSRIs, anti-Parkinson's medications (L-dopa), weight loss medications, tricyclics, tranquilizing drugs, antihistamines, cold medications, cancer chemotherapy, or antibiotic medications. In addition, it may strengthen the effect of certain tranquilizers and alcohol. Those who are at risk for heart disease or stroke, or those who have high blood pressure, also should abstain from 5-HTP until they've consulted their doctor.

GINKGO BILOBA

Approximately 200 million years old, Ginkgo biloba is the last surviving member of the ginkgo family *(Ginkgoaceae)*. Most gingko plants growing in North America and Europe were destroyed during the last ice age, but in Asia a small population in Northern China managed to survive. Now dubbed by herbalists around the world as the "living fossil," ginkgo has been used in Chinese botanical medicine for over 5,000 years and has been cultivated as a sacred herb.

The common name "ginkgo" is a phonetic pronunciation of a Japanese word for tree. The species name *biloba* refers to two distinct lobes of the leaves, which resemble a fan.[17] Today, some wild gingko trees can be located in China and Japan growing in front of ancient temples. In the wild, the tree can reach a height of more than one hundred feet, grow three to four feet in diameter, and live more than one thousand years. However, most of these trees seen throughout the Orient and other parts of the world—including the United States—are ornamental trees, frequently growing along sidewalks that line city streets.

For medicinal purposes, Ginkgo biloba has been developed into a standardized extract to ensure the potency of the major active chemicals in the ginkgo leaves. The extract is prepared to ensure 24 percent flavoneglycosides and 6 percent terpene lactones. According to a 1992 article in *The Lancet,* the flavoneglycosides are responsible for the plant's antioxidant activity, and the terpenoids are recognized for their platelet-activating factor (PAF) inhibition.

The reason for the herb's popularity is its demonstrated influence on cerebral vascular insufficiency. In Germany, ginkgo is licensed for the treatment of cerebral dysfunction for symptoms including difficulty with memory, dizziness, tinnitus, headaches, and emotional instability coupled with anxiety. The herb is also used as a supportive treatment for hearing loss resulting from cervical syndrome, as well as for peripheral arterial circulatory disturbances. Furthermore, ginkgo is frequently recommended in the treatment of Alzheimer's disease, acute memory loss, stroke prevention and recovery, prevention of memory loss, and promotion of cognitive function. For these reasons, many elderly people find ginkgo a particularly attractive supplement.

Ginkgo has also proved effective in the treatment of depression. Double-blind studies have demonstrated the extract's ability to enhance mood, especially for those with reduced brain circulation, again, making it more effective and popular with elderly people. One clinical double-blind study consisted of forty elderly patients suffering from depression (ages ranging from fifty-one to seventy-eight years of age), each of whom did not benefit from the standard prescription drugs for depression. In the study, half of the patients were administered 80 mg of Ginkgo biloba extract (GBE) and the other half a placebo, three times per day for four weeks. Utilizing the Hamilton Depression Scale as a guide to assess the patients' progress, the score in the GBE group was reduced 50 percent, from a score of 14 to 7. In contrast, the placebo group barely showed a 9 percent improvement, moving only from 14 to 13.[18] This study verifies ginkgo's antidepressive influence.

Another study yielded further evidence of ginkgo's antidepressant influence when researchers examined levels of serotonin receptors in young (four-months old) and old (twenty-four months old) rats. At the beginning of the study it was noted that the older rats had a lower percentage of serotonin binding sites on brain cells—as age increases changes in brain chemistry occur, such as the reduction in the number of serotonin receptors—this in turn undoubtedly may affect our disposition. The rats were administered daily doses of Ginkgo biloba extract and it was discovered that with the administration of GBE, older rats demonstrated an increased level of serotonin binding sites—approximately 33 percent more sites than seen at the beginning of the study. The same effect, however, was not found in younger rats; in fact, no changes were noted. Scientists concluded that GBE may help in the obstruction of the loss of serotonin receptors due to age, consequently effectively aiding the relief of depressive disorders in the elderly.

It is important to understand that ginkgo does not increase the level of neurotransmitters in the brain, but instead increases the number of serotonin receptors. The results of the study indicate that for the elderly the herb may be of significant clinical use when taken in combination with St. John's wort. The dosage used in the studies was 80 mg of standardized GBE three times per day, a dosage higher than the 40 mg three times per day, or 60 mg twice per day recommended for general users. Side effects and adverse reactions to ginkgo are rare, mild gastrointestinal discomfort being the most common although still very rare. In forty-four double-blind studies involving 9,772 patients who took ginkgo, only twenty-one suffered from gastrointestinal disturbances—only 00.21percent![19]

Most clinical researchers suggest that ginkgo be taken for a minimum of four to six weeks. Because its effect appears to be cumulative, the longer ginkgo is administered, the more potent its effect.

OMEGA-3 FATTY ACIDS

Some clinical researchers are now informing the public that depression may be influenced by a lack of fish in the diet—or at least a lack of essential fatty acids called the omega-3 fatty acids that are plentiful in fish.

Essential fats are classified as polyunsaturated fatty acids, a class of fats essential to the functioning of the human body. These fats are considered "essential" because the body can not produce them by itself and, therefore, must rely on external sources for its supply, either through diet or nutritional supplementation. Linoleic (omega 6) and alpha-linoleic acid (omega 3) are the two essential fatty acids (EFAs) integral to every cell membrane in the body. They and their derivatives (other fatty acids, and gamma-linoleic acid, or GLA) are involved in such diverse bodily functions as circulation, reproduction, metabolism, and growth.

As just mentioned, fish provide a significant dietary source of omega-3 polyunsaturated fatty acids; cold water fish are especially high in these EFAs (that is, mackeral, herring, sardines, salmon, and tuna). If fish does not appeal to you, then flaxseed oil or hemp oil are also significant sources of omega-3 fatty acids, as are such seaweeds as nori, kombu, and hijiki.

Omega-3 fatty acids first appeared on the scene in the '80s when a team of scientists went to Greenland to study the Eskimo people there.

They were surprised to discover that despite a diet high in fat due to the amount of fatty fish eaten, Eskimos were less likely to suffer from heart disease than many other groups of people. The same observation was made of people from the island of Japan who consume far greater quantities of fish than do their contemporaries in the United States.

The benefits of omega-3 fatty acids make a long list. They include reduction of cholesterol and triglyceride in blood levels, anticoagulant action, reduction of high blood pressure, anti-inflammatory action, relief and management of arthritis symptoms, cancer prevention and treatment, and treatment for multiple sclerosis. Scientists now are claiming that these acids are beneficial in the treatment of depression as well.[20, 21]

Evidence supporting the omega-3 fatty acid and depression link can be found in a recent study published in the *American Journal of Clinical Nutrition*. The authors, researchers at the National Institute of Alcohol Abuse and Alcoholism, suggest that a lack of omega-3 fatty acids may be the reason for increasing rates of depression over the past century. They write that "societies consuming large amounts of fish and omega-3 fatty acids appear to have lower rates of depression."[22] One specific study cited that North American and European populations exhibited cumulative rates of depression ten times greater than the Taiwanese population whose diet included a large amount of fresh fish.

While it might be premature to say that omega-3 fatty acid supplementation is a treatment for depressive disorder, researchers postulate that, like the EFAs, they have the potential to reduce the risk of coronary artery disease and might lower the risk of developing depression. Additional points about omega-3 fatty acids to consider are the following:

- It is theorized that contributors to postpartum depression, as well as to the risk of depression in women of childbearing age, is due to a lack of essential fatty acids in the diet, particularly omega-3 fatty acids. In pregnancy these nutrients are depleted from the mother's bloodstream because they are vital to the nervous system of the growing fetus.
- The lack of polyunsaturated fatty acids in the diet may have an adverse effect on the brain chemicals associated with depressive states, including serotonin and norepinephrine. Any

of their functions, including reuptake or the amount produced, may be altered by polyunsaturated fat intake.
- In chronic alcoholism, omega-3 fatty acids are stripped from
  the membrane of nerve cells, possibly explaining, in part, the
  reasons for depressive disorders among alcoholics.
- Studies have found a strong correlation between depression
  and coronary artery disease. Countries eating more fatty acids
  had less risk of heart disease and of depression; those that ate
  less increased the risk for development of both.

Taking the Omega-3 Fatty Acids

As mentioned, the omega-3 EFAs come in a variety of forms ranging
from fish oils to flax- and hemp seed oils to seaweed. If eating fish is not
part of your daily diet, then consider taking supplements. Supplements
are commonly available at health food stores and are relatively inexpensive to purchase. They run anywhere from five dollars per month to
twenty dollars per month, the cost, of course, depending on quality and
quantity purchased, and the store's location. Because potency of these
supplements varies across the board, follow the directions printed on the
label.

   *Note: Most fish oil contains EPA, a fatty acid that acts as a blood thinner;
therefore, pregnant women, infants, and the elderly should not take this
supplement. Diabetics should seek approval from their doctor before supple-
menting their diets with fish oils.*

PHENYLALANINE AND TYROSINE

There are twenty-two different forms of amino acids and all are required
to build the many various proteins of the body. The body must either
make proteins internally or have them supplied from an external source
via the diet. Proteins that the human body does not manufacture (of
which there are nine) fall into a category called *essential amino acids*.
Without these essential amino acids the body is unable to build the full
range of proteins in amounts necessary for the growth and maintenance
of various tissues. The body is able to synthesize the other nineteen
amino acids, which are called *nonessential amino acids*. Although these
amino acids are termed *nonessential*, they are absolutely integral to

health, as are the *essential,* because all proteins are constructed from arrangements of both essential and nonessential amino acids.[23]

Recent amino acid research has determined that amino acids are necessary for healthy brain functioning. They operate as forerunners for neurotransmitters and other mood-regulating chemicals, and so the lack of amino acids in the daily diet may account for depressive states. Daily supplementation of these building blocks of protein might actually help reverse a state of depression. Clinical researchers have concentrated on the role of three specific amino acids directly related to mood levels: tryptophan, phenylalanine, and tyrosine. We already have covered tryptophan when we discussed the supplement 5-HTP and its serotonin connection earlier in the chapter. If the name of the amino acid phenylalanine sounds faintly familiar, it is because it is an ingredient in the artificial sweetener aspartame, commonly referred to as NutraSweet, that is used in many sugar-free foods and beverages. While phenylalanine and tyrosine have not been the subject of as many studies as tryptophan, thus far they have been shown to be of significant use in the treatment of depression for some individuals.

Phenylalanine

Phenylalanine—which is converted into tyrosine in the body—is believed to play an integral role in the production of two major neurotransmitters: dopamine and norepinephrine. Phenylalanine is available in three distinct forms, D-, L-, and DL-phenylalanine. The last in the trio, called DLPA for short, is a mixed version of the first two, D- and L-phenylalanine. Both D- and L-phenylalanines have been evaluated in studies, sometimes mixed together and other times separate, but the DLPA is preferable because it is thought to cross the BBB. While both versions are chemically identical, they are structurally opposite, which explains their variation in action. One older study conducted in 1978 documented the effectiveness of DLPA versus the standard antidepressant imipramine in the treatment of depression. The trial consisted of sixty patients and was run double blind for thirty days. The sixty patients were split into two groups, thirty patients placed in the DLPA group, thirty others in the imipramine group. Daily doses of 100 mg of each medicine were administered to the patients in either group.

The results showed that DLPA worked as well as the prescription item, with one significant difference: the DLPA was noted to be faster acting than imipramine.[24]

Another double-blind study comparing the effects of DLPA and imipramine also confirmed the clinical effectiveness of DLPA in the treatment of depression. A total of twenty-seven patients were tested, half of whom received 200 mg daily doses of DLPA, the other half of whom received 200 mg daily doses of imipramine. Again, the statistical results were equivalent. DLPA was observed to be equally as effective as the leading tricyclic. Yet another interesting study documented the effectiveness of DLPA on patients who did not respond to tricyclic and MAOI drugs. Seventeen of the twenty-three patients experienced a positive response.[25]

The use of DLPA has several contraindications. Pregnant and nursing women and individuals who suffer from diabetes, hypertension, and anxiety attacks are advised against taking DLPA. Those who suffer from the metabolic disease phenylketonuria (PKU) are also advised to avoid usage. The average dosage employed in the study and recommended by doctors is 200–400 mg per day, divided in three to four doses to be taken between meals and on an empty stomach.

L-Tyrosine

The other amino acid necessary to brain function is L-tyrosine, an essential amino acid and precursor to the neurotransmitters dopamine and norepinephrine. A lack of norepinehprine in the brain has been shown to affect mood regulation that may result in depression. Clinical studies utilizing the effectiveness of L-tyrosine were difficult to locate. Though it is sometimes recommended in clinical settings in the treatment of depression. It can be obtained in pill form or from the diet.

The average dosage of supplementation with L-tyrosine is 300–500 mg per day, divided into three doses. Like DLPA, it too is taken between meals on an empty stomach. Supplemental tyrosine should not be taken by people with thyroid disease (hyperthyroidism), melanoma, or those taking MAOIs or other mood regulating chemicals. Anyone taking prescription drugs should consult with their physician before administering both DLPA and L-tyrosine.

HOMEOPATHY FOR DEPRESSION AND ANXIETY

Earlier we discussed an alternative system of medicine referred to as *homeopathy* briefly discussing the homeopathic perspective on diagnosis and treatment, as well the remedies' unique manufacturing process (successive dilution followed by succussion) and mechanism of action. Also touched upon were the benefits of administering a homeopathically potentized form of St. John's wort in addition to a homeopathic St. John's wort tincture in the treatment of depressive, skin, and nerve disorders.

Although homeopathic hypericum is not utilized in the treatment of depressive disorder (with the exception of the tincture and the lowest potency remedies), there are several homeopathic remedies that are better indicated for the treatment of depression and anxiety and have been listed here, followed by a brief paragraph detailing their corresponding symptoms. As you read the following summarization of symptoms, you will notice that the key points of each remedy differ, though they are administered for the same condition. Unlike other natural medicinals, selecting a homeopathic remedy is dependent upon matching the symptoms of the individual—no matter how obscure they might be—to the remedy. Once a proper match is made, the treatment can begin.

Note: Very few clinical studies have been done with homeopathic remedies, therefore I am able to provide only limited scientific validation for the use of the following. Nonetheless, these remedies are widely used the world over and have become the mainstay treatment of many naturopaths.

Aconite: is the Latin name for the herb monkshood. This remedy is indicated for treating both emotional shock and anxiety. The Aconite individual is frightened, restless, and afraid that death is imminent. He or she is very agitated and may seem on the verge of collapse.

Arsenicum album: is the Latin name for the toxic mineral Arsenic. Toxic in its raw version, the homeopathic remedy poses no toxic threat due to the dilution process. This remedy is good for both short-term insomnia and anticipatory anxiety. The Arsenicum individual is mentally and physically very restless, waking up between midnight and two A.M., feeling shaken and disturbed. His or her anxiety might manifest itself in an obsessional concern with cleanliness, despite a feeling of overwhelming exhaustion. A good remedy for lack of energy, as well.

Ignatia: is the Latin name for the St. Ignatius Bean (another mood enhancing Saint!). It is indicated for highly emotional individuals who tend to be oversensitive, nervous, and capricious. The Ignatia individual may go through weeping spells that alternate with bouts of laughter. Everything riles the Ignatia personality—he or she is easily excited. Violent weeping is the central symptom to selecting Ignatia.[26]

Natrum muriaticum (or Natrum mur.): is the Latin name for sodium chloride, or salt. It is one of the finest remedies for the type of grief that is not adequately expressed, or cannot be expressed. The Natrum personalities may want to cry, but have difficulty doing so in front of others. They dislike consolation because it is likely to produce tears, and they feel better being alone.

Pulsatilla: is the Latin name for the wind flower. It is generally prescribed to females to treat grief or shock that leads to constant tearfulness. Unlike the Natrum muriaticum personality, the Pulsatilla individual exhibits a constant need for sympathy; she feels better when consoled. Though she may cry often, she feels somewhat relieved by it. Unlike the Natrum mur., the Pulsatilla person does not want to be left alone.

Staphysagria: is the Latin name for stavesacre. This remedy is recommended when the depressed individual exhibits continuous anger as a result of shock or bereavement. Because the anger has been denied its natural expression, it is channeled outward in bursts of furious energy. The Staphysagria personality is irritable, nervous, excitable, and violent. He or she is very sensitive, physically and emotionally.[27]

Each of these homeopathic remedies can be purchased at local health food stores at potencies ranging from 6X to 30X or 6C to 30C. The higher potencies such as 200X or 1M are available only through homeopathic and naturopathic physicians, homeopathic dispensaries, and some pharmacies. The high potency homeopathic remedies are worthwhile medicinals but should not be administered without professional supervision. The letters X and C represent different forms of homeopathic potencies. X represents the number "10," which is indicative of the one part substance to nine parts dilution. Similarly C represents the number "100", indicating one part substance to ninety-nine parts dilution.

The quality of homeopathic remedies varies greatly—some are very effective while others are outright worthless. While I carry many different homeopathic products in my dispensary, I am most impressed with the quality coming out of National Homeopathic Products. They are not found in health food stores, but primarily in doctor's offices. Their remedies are somewhat more expensive than some of the leading name brands, but their quality is superior.

THE B VITAMINS

The B vitamins are a class of water-soluble vitamins like vitamin C. Water soluble means they remain no longer than three days in various body tissues and, consequently, need to be replenished daily. Absorbed into the bloodstream through the intestines, any excess amounts that the body does not need are excreted through the urine. Taking unnecessarily large amounts of water-soluble vitamins results in what many doctors call "expensive urine." In contrast, fat soluble vitamins like A, D, and E are absorbed through the intestines with dietary fats and may be stored in the liver and fatty tissue for as long as several months. Sometimes they are even stored for as long as a year or more. Large quantities of these vitamins do not have to be taken daily; in fact, taking them in large amounts is potentially harmful.[28]

The B vitamins have been dubbed the "anti-stress" vitamins because they are noted for their effectiveness in maintaining normal brain function. In results similar to the clinical research performed with amino acids, scientists have verified that the B vitamins, when administered in adequate quantities—particularly vitamins B_6, B_{12}, and folic acid—may stave off depression and in some cases even reverse it. Furthermore, deficiencies of these vitamins in the body have been implicated as a potential cause of depressive illness.

Vitamin B_3

Vitamin B_3, or niacin, is credited with improving cerebral circulation. Scientists contend that subclinical bodily deficiencies in niacin may result in agitation and anxiety, as well as mental and physical sluggishness. To overcome symptoms of B_3 deficiency, physicians prescribe large doses of this vitamin.[29] Daily dosages of 1000 mg–2000 mg may elevate liver enzymes, causing liver damage.

Vitamin B_6

Vitamin B_6, also known as pyridoxine, participates in more than eighty biochemical reactions in the body, including the production of neurotransmitters central to mood regulation (that is, serotonin, norepinephrine, and dopamine). Dr. Michael Murray, author of *Natural Alternatives to Prozac*, suggests that persons who are being treated with Prozac might actually be suffering from a vitamin B_6 deficiency; when these persons are subsequently issued the vitamin B_6 in clinical therapy, they respond very well.[30] (B_6 is necessary for the manufacturing of serotonin out of the amino acid tryptophan.) B_6 also has proved useful for women suffering from premenstrual syndrome (PMS), a condition characterized by irritability, anxiety, mood swings, water retention, and headaches. The approximate adult daily dose is 50 mg to 100 mg. If you are contemplating using a higher dose, consult your physician. Doses of 500 mg or more may be toxic and result in neurological damage.

Folic Acid and B_{12}

Folic acid and B_{12} are two B vitamins that have a close relationship with one another and together are involved in many biochemical actions. Scientists have found that at least a third of patients suffering from depression or dementia exhibit deficiencies of folic acid.[31] Like folic acid, a vitamin B_{12} deficiency has also been implicated as a cause of depression, especially in the elderly,[32] but once the lack of either of these B vitamins is restored to healthy levels, the depressive states abate.

Other clinical studies with folic acid and B_{12} have mirrored these results. One such study documented how these B vitamins stimulated the formation of a brain compound called tetrahydrobiopterin (BH_4) and how B_{12}, folic acid, and vitamin C influence the synthesis of monoamines like serotonin. BH_4 "functions as an essential coenzyme in the activation of enzymes that manufacture monoamine neurotransmitters such as serotonin and dopamine from their corresponding amino acids."[33]

The average dosage for folic acid is 200–800 mcgs per day, although some of the studies used doses as high as 15–50 mg in treating depression. Use of this vitamin in high doses is safe and nontoxic—except for individuals with epilepsy—but it is still recommended, as with any significant dietary change, that a physician be consulted. An excess of folate intake may mask a vitamin B_{12} deficiency, therefore, it is suggested that both B vitamins be taken simultaneously. The suggested daily dose of B_{12} is 100–800 mcg per day, although more may be taken safely since this vitamin is safe and nontoxic in oral doses. In addition to these specific B vitamins, a B-complex should be taken because of close interrelationship of the vitamins in the group with the metabolic processes of converting food into tissue or for the production of energy.

CHAPTER 8

GET READY, GET SET, GO!
Commonly Asked Questions

*The highest ideal of cure is rapid, gentle, and permanent
restoration of the health, or removal and annihilation of the
disease in its whole extent, in the shortest, most reliable, and
most harmless way, on easily comprehensible principles.*

Samuel Hahnemann, *Organon of Medicine*

If you are interested in locating more information about St. John's wort
refer to the organizations listed in the back of the book. In addition the
endnotes identify many journal articles that have published information
on hypericum.

Here are answers to some of the most commonly asked questions
about St. John's wort.

Q. Is hypericum addictive? Will I be able to quit once I have started?

A. None of the clinical research conducted to date has shown St. John's
wort to be addictive. It has been taken safely in Europe for thousands of
years with no history of reported addictions. The German Commission
E did not warn of addiction in its official monograph, nor did the
authors of the St. John's wort monograph of the American Herbal
Pharmacopoeia.

*Q. I am afraid I may develop a tolerance for hypericum. Will it lose its
effectiveness over time?*

A. Whenever any medication is taken for a considerable length of time, there is always the possibility that one may develop a tolerance for it. The easiest way to remedy this is to discontinue its use temporarily or to increase the dosage. Visit your physician to determine the next step in your treatment. As discussed in chapter 2, depression may have both biological and psychological roots. You should investigate some of the other possible factors that may be causing depression.

Q. What happens if I forget to take my dose for the day?

A. The effects of St. John's wort are cumulative. With every dose, concentrations of hypericin continue to build up in the brain. Missing one or two doses will not have a radical effect on the treatment program; sufficient levels of hypericin will not be lost. However, if you forget to take St. John's wort for a considerably longer period of time, perhaps two weeks, then the levels of hypericin will have been drastically reduced. When you resume taking the herb, you may not feel its beneficial effects until hypericin levels reach their steady state once again. This could take several weeks.

Q. Can I overdose on hypericum?

A. AIDS patients who were given roughly ten times the average recommended dose experienced a photosensitizing reaction to St. John's wort, in the form of rashes and itching. When the medication was discontinued, however, the symptoms quickly went away. The average user need not worry since the standard dosage is significantly lower. No deaths have ever been attributed to St. John's wort in its long history of use.

Q. What happens if a member of my family accidentally ingests several of my St. John's wort capsules? Will there be a problem?

A. One dose of two, three, four, or ten capsules of St. John's wort will not harm anyone who has accidentally ingested the herb. Hypericum is commonly taken for brief periods of time for its other, immune-stimulating, antiviral, anti-inflammatory properties. Unless the individual has a particular allergic reaction to St. John's wort, there should be no problems. If, however, you feel uncomfortable with the situation, contact your doctor or the poison control center for advice.

Q. If I am traveling in the United States or abroad, will I be able to purchase St. John's wort over the counter?

A. Because St. John's wort is regulated as a dietary supplement, you will not need a prescription for its purchase in the United States. It is widely available in pharmacies, health food stores, supermarkets, and warehouse clubs. If you are going abroad, however, different rules apply in different countries. In Mexico, it is sold over the counter. In parts of Europe, it is sold over the counter as well.

Q. Will I be able to drive my car safely if I am taking St. John's wort? I am afraid that I will fall asleep at the wheel.

A. Unlike certain psychoactive medications, which have the tendency to affect motor or thought skills and impair judgment, hypericum does not affect the user in this way. It is not dangerous to drive a motor vehicle or operate hazardous machinery while taking St. John's wort. Although the herb is administered in the treatment of insomnia, it does not produce drowsiness.

Q. How does alcohol interact with St. John's wort? Can I drink a glass of beer or wine while on the herbal medication?

A. In a double-blind study, patients were given hypericum and alcohol simultaneously to determine the potential effects of their interaction. Investigators found that a moderate amount of alcohol had no negative impact on cognitive functioning. Thus, it appears that a glass of beer or wine will not have any negative effect on the hypericum user. Before you decide to take a drink, however, check with your physician. Your physician may recommend that you eliminate or limit your intake of alcohol while under treatment for depression. Alcoholics and severe depressives should, of course, abstain from alcohol altogether.

Q. My doctor is not familiar with St. John's wort for the treatment of depression. What should I do?

A. Since St. John's wort has received so much media coverage, your doctor may have at least heard of the herbal antidepressant. If he or she has not, do not fret. Some doctors are not familiar with herbal medicine. My first suggestion is to give your doctor a copy of *The Prozac Alternative*.

In addition, refer to the endnote section and provide your doctor with copies of significant studies reported in the *British Medical Journal* and the *Journal of Geriatric Psychiatry and Neurology*. These should be easily obtainable at your local library or science library. As mentioned earlier, you might want to consult a naturopathic doctor or qualified herbalist for expert advice. They should be well-informed about the herb and its therapeutic action.

Q. Will St. John's wort increase energy levels?

A. Low energy, fatigue, and lack of motivation are common symptoms of depression. When depression lifts, however, a newfound sense of energy usually returns to the individual. Taking hypericum for its anti-depressant effects may restore your normal energy level, but St. John's wort does not function as a stimulant. Popping a hypericum capsule when you are dragging at the end of a day or before you head out for a night on the town will not increase your energy levels.

Q. What if I feel normal but want to be happier?

A. The old saying, "If it ain't broke, don't fix it," applies here. St. John's wort has a normalizing effect on the user. It will help a depressed person lose his or her depressed feelings, but it will not affect a normal, healthy person in the same way. Similarly, aspirin will reduce the temperature of someone with a fever, but it will not lower normal body temperature.

St. John's Wort Suppliers

A great number of companies manufacture and sell both the raw, crude version and the standardized extract of St. John's wort. The following is a list of various reputable sources in the nutritional supplement industry. The author does not endorse these companies, but lists them for the reader's convenience.

Bio-Botanica, Inc.
75 Commerce Dr.
Hauppauge, NY 11788
516-231-5522
800-645-5720

BNG Enterprises
1809 W. 4th St.
Tempe, AZ 85281
602-967-9115
800-445-0161

Country Life Vitamins
101 Corporate Drive
Hauppage, NY 11788
800-645-5768

Eclectic Institute
14385 SE Lusted Road
Sandy, OR 97055
503-668-4120
800-332-4372

Enzymatic Therapy, Inc.
P.O. Box 22310
Green Bay, WI 54305
414-469-1313
800-558-7372

Futurebiotics, Inc.
145 Ricefield Lane
Hauppauge, NY 11788
516-273-6300

Natrol, Inc.
20731 Marilla St.
Chatsworth, CA 91311
800-326-1520

Naturally Vitamin Supplements
14851 N. Scottsdale Road
Scottsdale, AZ 85254
602-991-0200
800-899-4499

Nature's Herbs
600 E. Quality Drive
American Fork,   UT 84003
800-HERBALS

Nature's Way
10 Mountain Springs Parkway
Springville, UT 84663
801-489-1500
800-926-8883

Nutraceutical Corporation (Soloray and Kal)
P.O. Box 681869
Park City, UT 94068
800-669-8877

Schiff Products, Inc.
1960 South 4250 West
Salt Lake City, UT 84104
801-972-0300

Solgar Nutrition Research Center
Ocean Pines
11017 Mankin Meadows Lane
Berlin, MD 21811
410-641-7411

Thompson Nutritional Products
4301 N.E. 12th Terrace
Ft. Lauderdale, FL 33334
800-421-1192

HERBAL EDUCATION PROGRAMS AND READING LIST

For further information on the responsible use of medicinal plants contact these institutions:

American Botanical Council
P.O. Box 201660
Austin, TX 78720
800-373-7105
512-331-8868

American Botanical Council is a nonprofit education and research organization, and a copublisher of *HerbalGram* with the Herb Research Foundation. In addition, they publish booklets on herbs and reprints of scientific articles.

American Herbal Pharmacopoeia
P.O. Box 5159
Santa Cruz, CA 95063-5159
408-461-6318

American Herbal Pharmacopoeia promotes the art and science of healing, supplying knowledge of herbal medicine to professionals and lay persons in the health care field. Publishers of herbal monographs.

The American Herbalists Guild
P.O. Box 1683
Sequel, CA 95073

The American Herbalists Guild's members range from clinical prac-
tioners to ethnobotanists who are committed to the advancing field of
medical herbalism. They can provide a directory of schools and teachers.

Herb Reserch Foundation
1007 Pearl Street, Suite 200
Boulder, CO 80302
800-748-2617

The Herb Research Foundation provides research materials for con-
sumers, physicians, pharmacists, scientists, and the health food industry.
They are copublishers of *HerbalGram* with the American Botanical
Council.

HerbalGram
American Botanical Council
P.O. Box 201660
Austin, Texas 78720
512-331-8868
800-272-7105 (Phone orders)
512-331-1924 (Fax)

HerbalGram is the quarterly magazine of the American Botanical Council
and the Herb Research Foundation. The magazine includes medical
and scientific updates on herbs, feature articles, changes in legal and
regulatory matters, conferences, reviews on medicinal plants, book reviews, quality control, and more.

Foster's Botanical & Herb Reviews
P.O. Box 106
Eureka Springs, AK 72632
501-253-7442 (Fax)

Foster's Botanical & Herb Reviews is one of the older publications in the
field dedicated to a wide range of herbal topics, including media coverage, internal developments, regulatory issues, quality control, research,
health crazes, and more.

Medical Herbalism
P.O. Box 33080
Portland, OR 97233
503-242-9815

Published six times per year, *Medical Herbalism* is a newsletter written primarily for practitioners of botanical medicine.

Association of Natural Medicine Pharmacists (ANMP)
8369 Champs d'Elysses
Forestville, CA 95436
707-887-1351

The Association of Natural Medicine Pharmacists raises awareness of botanical medicine and provides educational materials on natural medicines to practicing pharmacists.

General Resources
For Depression

**Depression/Awareness, Recognition and
Treatment Education Program (DART)**
National Institute of Mental Health
Room 7C-02
5600 Fishers Lane
Rockville, MD 20857
800-421-4211

The Depression/Awareness, Recognition and Treatment Education
Program provides an information line as part of the National Institutes
of Health, and offers a series of brochures and pamphlets on a variety of
subjects free of charge.

National Mental Health Association
1021 Prince Street
Alexandria, VA 22314-2971
800-969-NMHA

The National Mental Health Association provides information on
various mental health topics free of charge. It also offers referrals to
mental health providers and a directory for local mental health
associations.

The National Foundation for Depressive Illness

P.O. Box 2257
New York, NY 10116
800-239-1263

Information on depressive illness and a referral list of physicians in local area is available through The National Foundation for Depressive Illness, a nonprofit, charitable organization.

National Depressive and Manic Depressive Association

730 North Franklin Street, Suite 501
Chicago, IL 60610
800-826-3632

The National Depressive and Manic Depressive Association educates families, patients, professionals, and the public concerning the nature of depressive and manic depressive illnesses as treatable medical diseases. They encourage self-help for patients and families, and work to eliminate discrimination and stigma, to improve access to care, and to advocate for research towards the illumination of their illnesses. A nonprofit organization.

American Association of Naturopathic Physicians

2366 Eastlake Avenue, Suite 322
Seattle, WA 98102
206-323-7610

The American Association of Naturopathic Physicians provides referrals to a nationwide network of accredited or licensed practitioners. It publishes a quarterly letter for both professionals and the general public. (Sample copy available upon request.)

American Holistic Medical Association

4101 Lake Boone Trail, Suite 201
Raleigh, NC 27607
919-787-4916

The American Holistic Medical Association is an organization of holistic M.D.s and D.O.s who pratice integrated medicine. (Referrals to practitioners in your area are given.)

The Center for the Improvement of Human Functioning International
3100 North Hillside Avenue
Wichita, KS 67219-3904
316-682-3100

The Center for the Improvement of Human Functioning is a medical, research, and educational facility specializing in the treatment of chronic illness and is considered to be at the forefront of nutritional medicine. Seminars, training programs for health care providers, and a monthly newsletter are available.

NOTES

CHAPTER 1

1. Edmund L. Andrews, "In Germany Humble Herb is a Rival to Prozac," *New York Times*, 9 September 1997.
2. Jane E. Brody, "Personal Health," *New York Times*, 17 September 1997.
3. Sue Miller, "A Natural Mood Booster: More and more therapists are recommending an herb called St. John's wort to treat mild depression. Does it work?," *Newsweek* 129, no.18 (5 May 1997): 74–75.
4. Michael Jenike, Editorial, *Journal of Geriatric Psychiatry and Neurology* 7, Suppl.1 (1994): S3.
5. Ibid.
6. Barbara and Peter Theiss, *The Family Herbal: A Guide to Natural Health Care for Yourself and Your Children from Europe's Leading Herbalists* (Rochester, Vermont: Healing Arts Press, 1993), 120–24.
7. Christopher Hobbs, "St. John's Wort, Hypericum Perforatum LA Review," *HerbalGram* 18/19, (1989): 24–33.
8. Ibid.
9. Micheal Castleman, *The Healing Herbs* (Emmaus, Pennsylvania: Rodale Press, 1991), 7–8.
10. Harold H. Bloomfield, Michael Nordfors, and Peter McWilliams, *Hypericum and Depression: Can Depression Be Successfully Treated with a Safe, Inexpensive, Medically Proven Herb Available without a Prescription?* (Los Angeles: Prelude Press, 1996), 18.

CHAPTER 2

1. N. R. Farnsworth et al. "Medicinal Plants in Therapy," *Bulletin of the World Health Organization* 63, no.6 (1985): 965–81. Reprinted in *Alternative Medicine, the Definitive Guide*.
2. Burton Goldberg Group, *Alternative Medicine, the Definitive Guide* (Puyallup, Washington: Future Medicine Publishing, Inc., 1993), 254.
3. Ibid., 3–16.
4. Michael T. Murray, *The Healing Power of Herbs: The Enlightened Person's Guide to the Wonders of Medicinal Plants* (Rocklin, CA: Prima Publishing, 1995), 1.
5. Herb Trade Association, *Definition of "Herb"* (Austin, Texas: Herb Trade Association), 1977.
6. Burton Goldberg Group, *Alternative Medicine, the Definitive Guide*, 254.
7. Murray, *The Healing Power of Herbs*, 3–16.
8. P. P. Principe, "The economic significance of plants and their constituents as drugs," *Econ Med Plant Res* 3 (1989): 1–17. Reprinted in *The Healing Power of Herbs*.
9. Mark Blumenthal, "Herbal Update: Testing Botanicals," *Whole Foods* 20, no. 7 (1997): 52.
10. Murray, *The Healing Power of Herbs*, 2–3.
11. Larry Katzenstein, *Secrets of St. John's Wort: Treat Depression Naturally with St. John's wort* (New York: St. Martin's Paperbacks, 1998), 21.
12. Marcia Zimmerman, "Guide to Phytonutrients, Food as Medcine," *Delicious!* 13, no. 8 (1997): 14.
13. Steven Foster, "The Challenges of Competition," *Health Foods Business* 43, no. 8 (1997): 20.
14. Murray, *The Healing Power of Herbs*, 12–13.
15. Nature's Answer, Inc. *Holistically Balanced Standardized Liquid Herbal Extracts* (Hauppauge, NY, 1997), 9.
16. Mark Blumenthal, *Whole Foods*, 54.
17. Ibid.

CHAPTER 3

1. Diane Hales, *Depression: Psychological Disorders and Their Treatment* (New York: Chelsea House Publishers, 1989), 20.
2. Ronald R. Fieve, *Prozac* (New York: Avon Books, 1994), 24.
3. Marvin E. Licky and Barbara Gordon, *Medicine and Mental Illness: The Use of Drugs in Psychiatry* (New York: W. H. Freeman and Co., 1991), 46.

4. William S. Appleton, *Prozac and the New Antidepressants: What You Need To Know About Prozac, Zoloft, Paxil, Wellbutrin, Effexor, Serzone, Luvox and More* (New York: Penguin Group, 1997), 21.

5. Sandra Salsman, *Depression, Questions you have . . . Answers you need* (Allentown, Penn.: People's Medical Society, 1995), 19.

6. Wray Herbert, "Politics of Biology," *U.S. News & World Report*, 122: 15 (1997), 72–80.

7. Diane Hales, *Depression*, 48.

8. Marvin E. Lickey and Barbara Gordon, *Medicine and Mental Illness*, 16.

9. Ibid.

10. Scott K. Veggeberg, *Medication of the Mind* (New York: Henry Holt & Company, 1996), 12.

11. Robert M. Julien, *A Primer of Drug Action: A Concise, Nontechnical Guide to the Actions, Uses, and Side Effects of Psychoactive Drugs* (New York: W. H. Freeman and Company, 1995), 189.

12. Sandra Salsman, *Depression*, 76.

13. James J. Rybacki and James W. Long, *The Essential Guide to Prescription Drugs*, 784.

14. William S. Appleton, *Prozac and the New Antidepressants*, 30.

15. Richard Restak, *Medication of the Mind*, 9.

16. Wray Herbert, "Politics of Biology," *U.S. News & World Report*, 77.

17. Paul H. Wender and Donald F. Klein. *Mind, Mood, and Medicine: A Guide to the New Biopsychiatry* (Toronto: McGraw-Ryerson Ltd., 1981), 329.

CHAPTER 4

1. Edmund L. Andrews, *New York Times*.

2. Upton, R. et al., *American Herbal Pharmacopoeia and Therapeutic Compendium St. John's wort: Hypericum Perforatum*. Santa Cruz, 1997, 9.

3. Ibid, 12.

4. Peter De Smet and Willem A. Nolen, "St. John's wort as an antidepressant," *British Medical Journal* 313, no. 7052 (1996): 241–42.

5. K. Linde, G. Ramirez, C. D. Mulrow, A. Pauls, W. Weidenhammer, and D. Melchart, "St. John's wort for depression—an overview and metanalysis of randomized clinical trials," *British Medical Journal* 313, no. 7052 (1996):253–58.

6. Jerry Cott, "Natural Product Formulations Available in Europe for Psychotropic Indications," *Psychopharmacology Bulletin* 31, no. 4 (1995): 745–51.

7. Edmund L. Andrews, *New York Times*.

8. Ibid.

9. Jerry Cott, "Medicinal plants and Dietary Supplements: Sources for Innovative Treatments or Adjuncts," *Psychopharmacology Bulletin* 31, no. 4 (1995): 131–35.

10. O. Suzuki, Y. Katsumata, M. Oya, S. Bladt, and H. Wagner, "Inhibition of monamine oxidase by hypericin," *Planta Medica* 50 (1984): 272–74.

11. S. Bladt and H. Wagner, "Inhibition of MAO by fractions and constituents of hypericum extract," Journal *of Geriatric Psychiatry and Neurology* 7, Suppl. 1 (1994): S57–S59.

12. L. Demisch, J. Holzl, B. Golnik, Kacynarczyk, "Identification of MAO-type-A inhibitors in *Hypericum perforatum* L. (hyperforat)," *Pharmacopsychiatry*, no. 22 (1989): 194.

13. Harold H. Bloomfield, Michael Nordfors, and Peter McWilliams, *Hypericum and Depression*, 76.

14. M. Nordfors and P. Harvig, "St.John's wort against depression in favour again," *Lakartidningen* 94. :25 (1997): 2365-2367.

15. H. Winterhof, V. Butterweck, A. Nahstedt, H. G. Gumbinger, V. Schulz, S. Erping, F. Bosshammer, and A. Wieligmann, "Phytopharmaka in Forschung unf klinischer Anwendung," *Loew D*: 1995 Steinkopff Verlag GmbH & Co.KG. Darmstadt S39–52. Reprinted in *Hypericum and Depression*, 184–85.

16. Ibid.

17. E. Ernst, "St. John's wort as antidepressive therapy," *Fortschr Med* 113, no. 25 (1995): 354–55.

18. B. Witte, G. Harrer, T. Kaptan, H. Podzuweit, U. Schmidt, "Treatment of depressive symptoms with a high concentration hypericum preparation. A multicenter placebo-controlled double-blind study," *Fortschr Med* 113, no. 28 (1995): 404–8.

19. Harold H. Bloomfield, Michael Nordfors, and Peter McWilliams, *Hypericum and Depression*, 101.

20. Barbara and Peter Theiss, *The Family Herbal*, 119.

21. C. Reh, P. Laux, N. Schenk, "Hypericum extract in the treatment of depression: An effective alternative," *Therapiewoche*, no. 42 (1992): 1576–81. Reprinted in *Hypericum and Depression*, 154–56.

22. Kenneth Bender, "St. John's Wort Evaluated as Herbal Antidepressant," *Psychiatric Times*, October 1996, 58.

23. R. Upton et al. *American Herbal Pharmacopoeia and Therapeutic Compendium St. John's wort: Hypericum Perforatum*. Santa Cruz, 1997, 22.

24. Ibid, 19.

25. H. Winterhoff et al., S39–52. Reprinted in *Hypericum and Depression*, 154–56.

26. Harold H. Bloomfield, Michael Nordfors, and Peter McWilliams, *Hypericum and Depression*, 166.

27. B. Thiele, I. Brink, M. Ploch, "Modulation of cytokine expression by hypericum extract," *Journal of Geriatric Psychiatry and Neurology* 7, Suppl. 1 (1994): S60–62.

28. W. E. G. Muller and R. Rossol., *Journal of Geriatric Psychiatry and Neurology*, S29–33.

29. Ibid.

30. B. Martinez, S. Kasper, S. Ruhrmann, and H. J. Moller, "Hypericum in the Treatment of Seasonal Affective Disorders," *Journal of Geriatric Psychiatry and Neurology* 7, Suppl. 1 (1994): S29–33

31. Ibid.

32. L. Demisch, J. Nispel, T. Sielaff, P. Gebhart, C. Kohler, and B. Pflug, "Nocturnal melatonin and cortisol secretions before and after subchronic administration of Hyperforat," Abstract from the AGNP symposium, Nuremberg 1991. Reprinted in *Hypericum and Depression*, 154–56.

33. Russel J. Reiter and Jo Robinson, *Your Body's Natural Wonder Drug, Melatonin* (New York: Bantam Books, 1995), 134–36.

34. Ibid.

35. Marilyn Chase, "Studies are Shedding New Light on Therapy for Winter Depression," *The Wall Street Journal,* December 15, 1997.

36. Harold H. Bloomfield, Michael Nordfors, and Peter McWilliams, *Hypericum and Depression,* 100.

37. H. Woelk, G. Gurkard, and J. Grunwald, "Benefits and Risks of the Hypericum Extract L1 160: Drug Monitoring Study with 3250 Patients," *Journal of Geriatric Psychiatry and Neurology* 7, Suppl. 1 (1994): S34–38.

38. Ibid.

39. Ibid.

40. E. U. Vorbach, W. D. Hubner, and K. H. Arnoldt, "Effectiveness and Tolerance of the Hypericum Extract L1 160 in Comparison with Imipramine: Randomized Double-Blind Study with 135 Outpatients," *Journal of Geriatric Psychiatry and Neurology* 7, Suppl. 1 (1994): S19–23.

41. Harold H. Bloomfield, Michael Nordfors, and Peter McWilliams, *Hypericum and Depression,* 124–30.

42. Robert M. Julien, *A Primer of Drug Action,* 6–21

43. P. S. Chung, R. E. Saxton, M. B. Paiva, C. K. Rhee, J. Soudant, A. Mathey, C. Foote, and D. J. Castro, "Hypericin uptake in rabbits and nude mice transplanted with human squamous cell carcinomas: Study of a new sensitizer for laser phototherapy," *Laryngscope* 104, no. 12 (1994): 1471–76. Reprinted in *Hypericum and Depression, 169–72.*

44. "St. John's wort (Hypericum perforatum, A Breakthrough Herb," *NNFA Today* 11, no. 10 (1997): 7.

CHAPTER 5

1. According to Ayurvedic medicine, the whole herb imparts prana, the life force. This is supposed to be altered in standardized extracts. Some physicians may prefer the raw herb to the standardized extract, or at least they will add the whole herb to the standardized extract.
2. The product is Jarsin 300. It is the most popoular selling form of St. John's wort on the European market today. Lichtwer Pharma, the company who pushed for research on the herb, is responsible for the manufacturing of Jarsin 300.
3. Alan Christianson, interview by Ran Knishinsky. January 15, 1998.
4. Harold H. Bloomfield, Michael Nordfors, and Peter McWilliams, *Hypericum and Depression*, 139.
5. The greater number of side effects in the placebo groups are probably due to the depressive disorders that have gone untreated. But, it is very rare that the response to side effects in the placebo group is greater than the test group. Undoubtedly, hypericum has an extremely mild side-effect profile and appears to be effective.
6. Steven Bratman, *Beat Depression with St. John's wort* (Rocklin, CA: Prima Publishing, 1997), 2.
7. V. Mcauliffe et al., 1993. "A phase I dose escalation study of synthetic hypericin in HIV infected patients," *National Conference Human Retroviruses Related to Infection* (1st), 159. From Steven Bratman, *Beat Depression with St. John's wort*, 90.
8. Alfred Goodman Gilman, Theodore W. Rall, Alan S. Nies, and Palmer Taylor, *The Pharmacological Basis of Therapeutics*, (New York: Macmillan Publishing Company, 1993), 51.
9. Jonathan Zeuss, *The Natural Prozac Program: How to use St. John's wort, the Antidepressant Herb* (New York: Three Rivers Press, 1997), 77.
10. Steven Bratman, *Beat Depression with St. John's wort*, 94.

CHAPTER 6

1. D. Muruelo, G. Lavie, and D. Lavie, "Therapeutic agents with dramatic antiretroviral activity and little toxicity at effective doses: aromatic polycyclic diones hypericin and pseudohypericin," *Proceeding of the National Academy of Sciences of the United States of America* 85, no. 14 (1989): 5230–34.
2. R. Upton et al., *American Herbal Pharmacopoeia and Therapeutic Compendium St. John's wort: Hypericum Perforatum*. Santa Cruz, 1997, 22.

3. Michael T. Murray, *The Healing Power of Herbs*, 296.

4. R. Upton et al., *American Herbal Pharmacopoeia and Therapeutic Compendium St. John's wort: Hypericum Perforatum*. Santa Cruz, 1997, 10.

5. Ibid.

6. "St. John's wort," *Health Points* 3, no. 1 (Winter Issue 1998): 1.

7. Michael Moore, *Medicinal Plants of the Mountain West: A Guide to the Identification, Preparation, and Uses of Traditional Medicinal Plants Found in the Mountains, Foothills, and Upland Areas of the American West* (Albequerque: Museum of New Mexico Press, 1979), 45.

8. Barbara and Peter Theiss, *The Family Herbal*, 119–24.

9. R. Upton et al., *American Herbal Pharmacopoeia and Therapeutic Compendium St. John's wort: Hypericum Perforatum*. Santa Cruz, 1997, 24.

10. C. Barbagallo and G. Chisari, "Antimicrobial activity of three *Hypericum* species," *Filoterapia* 58 (1987): 175–77.

11. Ibid.

12. Michael D Lemonick, "The Killers All Around," *Time Magazine* 144, no. 11 (September 12, 1994): 62–69.

13. G. Rath et al., "Xanxthones from Hypericum Roeperanum," *Phytochemistry* 43, no. 2 (1996): 513–20.

14. C. Barbagallo and G. Chisari, *Filoterapia*, 175–77.

15. M. L. Tyler, *Homeopathic Drug Pictures* (London: Homeopathic Publishing Company, 1942), 399–406.

16. R. Upton et al., *American Herbal Pharmacopoeia and Therapeutic Compendium St. John's wort: Hypericum Perforatum*. Santa Cruz, 1997, 25.

17. Asa Hersoff, "Homeopathic Remedies for Arthritis," *Let's Live* 63, no. 4 (April 1994): 24–26.

18. Homeopathy has recently gained many followers in the United States, but has still not reached a level of popularity achieved by its natural counterparts (herbs, minerals, vitamins) in the health food industry. Though popular among naturopathic doctors here, its use is generally contested among orthodox physicians. This is because of its preparation process, one that runs dramatically counter to contemporary scientific theory. I am referring to the higher potencies beyond 12C, not the tinctures.

19. R. Upton et al., *American Herbal Pharmacopoeia and Therapeutic Compendium St. John's wort: Hypericum Perforatum*. Santa Cruz, 1997, 26.

20. W. T. Couldwell et al., "Hypericin: a potential antiglioma therapy," *Neurosurgery* 35, no. 4 (1994): 705–10.

21. Jonathan Zeuss, *The Natural Prozac Program*, 58–59.

22. B. Vukic-Gacic and D. Simic, "Identification of natural antimutagens with modulating effects on DNA repair," *Basic Life Sciences* 61 (1993): 269–77.

Endnote printed from Jonathan Zuess, *The Natural Prozac Program*.

23. R. Upton et al., *American Herbal Pharmacopoeia and Therapeutic Compendium St. John's wort: Hypericum Perforatum*. Santa Cruz, 1997, 24.

24. Ibid.

CHAPTER 7

1. Andrea Petersen, "The Making of an Herbal Superstar," *The Wall Street Journal* (26 February 1998.)

2. Vincent Lebot, Mark Merlin, and Lamont Lindstrom, *Kava, the Pacific Elixir: The Definitive Guide to its Ethnobotany, History, and Chemistry* (Rochester, Vermont: Healing Arts Press, 1997), 60–64.

3. Ibid., 119.

4. Chris Kilham, *Kava, Medicine Hunting in Paradise: The Pursuit of a Natural Alternative to Anti-Anxiety Drugs and Sleeping Pills* (Rochester, Vermont: Park Street Press, 1996), 56–57.

5. Vincent Lebot et al., *Kava, the Pacific Elixir*, 119–21.

6. Ibid.

7. Chris Kilham, *Kava, Medicine Hunting in Paradise*, 67.

8. Ibid., 100.

9. H. Volz and M. Kieser. "Kava-kava Extract WS1490 vs. Placebo in Anxiety Disorders—a Randomized Placebo-Controlled 25-Week Outpatient Trial," *Pharmopsychiatry* 30, no. 1 (1997): 1–5.

10. D. Lindenberg and H. Pitule-Schodel. "D,L-kavain in comparison with oxazepam in anxiety disorders. A double-blind study of clinical effectiveness." *Forschr. Med.* 108 (1990): 49–50, 53–54. Reprinted in *Natural Alternatives to Prozac*.

11. G. Warnecke. "Neurovegetative dystonia in the female climacteric. Studies on the clinical efficacy and tolerance of kava extract WS 1490." *Fortschr. Med.* 109 (1991): 120–22. Reprinted in *Natural Alternatives to Prozac*.

12. Geoffrey Cowley and Anne Underwood. "A Little Help From Serotonin: Could a single brain chemical hold the key to happiness, high social status and a nice, flat stomach?" *Newsweek*.

13. "With A Little Help From Serotonin: 5-HTP and Serotonin Deficiency Syndrome." Monthly sales/information flyer entitled *Nutricology: In Focus*. February 1998, 3.

14. Dean W. Manders. "The Curious Continuing Ban of L-Tryptophan: The Serotonin Connection," *Stop the FDA* (Menlo Park, California: Health Freedom Pulbications, 1992), 129–38.

15. Ibid.

16. M. Maes, A. Van Gastel, R. Ranjan, P. Blockx, P. Cosyn, H. Y. Meltzer, and R. Desnyder, "Stimulatory effects of L-5-hydroxytryptophan on postdexamethasone beta-endorphin levels in major depression," *Neuropsychopharmacology* 15, no. 4 (1996): 340–8.

17. Steven Foster, "Ginkgo, Leaves of Life," *Better Nutrition for Today's Living* 57, no. 8 (1995): 46–50.

18. Michael T. Murray, *Natural Alternatives to Prozac* (New York: William Morrow & Co., 1996), 160–62.

19. Ibid.

20 Michael T. Murray, "Fats and Oils as Medicine: Heal with Essential Fats," *Well Being Journal* 7, no. 2 (March/April 1998): 5.

21. Jack Challem, "Doctors Are Using Magnesium, Fish Oils, and Calcium For Heart Problems," *Let's Live* 62, no. 2 (February 1994): 14–16.

22. J. R. Hibbeln and N. Salem, "Dietary polyunsaturated fatty acids and depression: when cholesterol does not satisfy," *American Journal of Clinical Nutrition* 62 (1995): 1–9.

23. John A. Pope Jr., editor, *Health And Healing The Natural Way: Eating For Good Health,* (London: The Reader's Digest Association Limited, 1995), 30–31.

24. B. Heller, "Pharmacological and clinical effects of D-phenylalanine in depression and Parkinson's disease," *Noncatecholic Phenylethylamines, Part I* (New York: Marcel Dekker), 397–417.

25. Michael T. Murray, *Natural Alternatives to Prozac*, 172–73.

26. C. M. Boger, *A Synoptic Key of the Materia Medica* (New Delhi, India: B. Jain Publishers, Ltd., 1990), 211–12.

27. Ibid., 308–09.

28. John A. Pope Jr., editor, *Health And Healing The Natural Way*, 60–61.

29· Hyla Cass, *St. John's wort, Nature's Blues Buster: A Common Sense Guide To Understanding & Using St. John's wort* (Garden City Park, New York: Avery Press, 1998), 121.

30. Michael T. Murray, *Natural Alternatives to Prozac,* 120–21.

31. R. Crellin, T. Bottiglieri, and E. H. Reynolds, "Folates and psychiatric disorder. Clinical Potential," *Drugs* 45 (1993): 623–36. Using Michael Murray's *Natural Alternatives to Prozac* as a source.

32. Ibid., 118–19.

33. Ibid., 119.

INDEX